Curious Little World

A Self-Imposed Exile on St. Helena Island

Rex Bartlett

Toppermost Books
Gabriola Island, British Columbia

Library and Archives Canada Cataloguing in Publication

Bartlett, Rex, 1952-
    Curious little world : a self-imposed exile on St. Helena Island / Rex Bartlett.

ISBN 978-0-9783927-0-3

    1. Bartlett, Rex, 1952 – Homes and haunts – Saint Helena. 2. Saint Helena – Description and travel. I. Title.

    DT671.S2B37 2007   997.3
    C2007-904094-2

Toppermost Books
P.O. Box 319
Gabriola Island
British Columbia V0R 1X0

Printed in Canada

For Cynthia Laura Barefoot

kind, wise, loving and fun

ST. HELENA

CURIOUS LITTLE WORLD

Charles Darwin visited the Island of St. Helena in 1836. He wrote this:

"St. Helena, situated so remote from any continent, in the midst of a great ocean... excites our curiosity... It is a curious little world within itself..."

Acknowledgements

Thanks to: Cynthia Laura Barefoot, all family, Mike and Serena Thorpe, Cathleen Hjalmarson, Hank and Gail, Bonnie Cruse and Oliver Garus, David and Joan Mitchell, Chris Stewart, Lesley Choyce and Julia Swan for some helpful editorial suggestions, our good neighbours on Woody Ridge, and all the friendly Saints.

Apologies to family and friends who get mentioned in this book and to family and friends who don't.

Cover photos of St. Helena: by Mike Thorpe
Front cover: view out to sea from Botley's Lay
Back cover: view of Sugarloaf from James Bay

Photo of the author and Cynthia Barefoot:
by E.A.Barefoot

Map showing global position of St. Helena: courtesy of The Jamestown Tourist Office

Map of St. Helena: designed by Marian Jeremiah, courtesy of The Jamestown Tourist Office

Portrait of Napoleon on St. Helena: by Rex Bartlett

Portrait of Dot Leo: by Cynthia Barefoot

Cover design: by Cynthia Barefoot and Rex Bartlett

Contents

FOREWORD

by

Cynthia Laura Barefoot

You know how to read a book, don'tcha?
You just wiggle your eyes and turn the pages.

Chapter One

The Beginning

In my case it all began in complete ordinariness and I had no warning of what was to come. I was just a typical Canadian kid, spending my time peeking out from behind a tree, thinking I was a squirrel. Then I'd scamper over to another tree and repeat the process. The years flew by.

Next thing I knew I was an adult. But tragically, not a typical Canadian adult. I was a Canadian adult tormented by a fixed idea. I can't explain how this happened. It just did.

Here's what I thought: that Canada should never have been a Full-Time Country. That it should always have been a summer resort, closed during the off-season, and that each September all Canadians should migrate to some warm and sunny spot until June. I didn't think Canada should be *governed* by a Government. I thought it should be *run...* by The Parks Department.

To my way of thinking, putting a Full-Time Country where Canada is had been A Huge Mistake. I tried repeatedly to alert my fellow Canadians to the mistake we were all making, but it did no good. Nothing was done about anything. People just looked at me. I got blank looks. And looks of fear. I got looks of suspicion and occasionally I'd get a look of patronizing sympathy. Mostly I got looks of naked disgust.

So I'm aware that, by now, many proud and patriotic Canadians reading this may be starting to dislike me. They might be thinking that I'm some sorta twisted, chicken-hearted wussy-pussy... *somethin'-or-other*. But they lack a specific derogatory label for someone like me. So I will give it to them: "anti-winterist."

Yes.

I am a twisted, chicken-hearted wussy-pussy anti-winterist.

But lovely with it.

Chapter Two

Exile With a Smile

One day though, while ranting anti-winterism, I detected someone listening with a quiet enthusiasm. The listener was a beautiful woman.

Cynthia Laura Barefoot.

We were in the frozen city of Winnipeg, capital city of the frozen province of Manitoba, where we were both born. Winnipeg is often billed as "Canada's Coldest Capital City." The winter climate in Manitoba bears a very striking resemblance to that of Siberia, in Russia. The main difference between the two places is that in Russia, people are *banished* to a life in Siberia as a cruel punishment, whereas in Canada, people live in Manitoba *of their own free will.*

Cynthia and I fell in love.

Together we began to explore the anti-winterism theme in depth. We swiftly recognized that the migratory Canadian anti-winterist life is the exclusive domain of The Filthy Rich and The Golden Years Gang, the latter being Canadians who have worked and saved all their lives to be able to live out an anti-winterist retirement.

Migratory anti-winterism involves the expense of owning or renting two residences; one in Canada, and one in, say, Florida, or the Caribbean, as well as the expense of the annual migrations. This extravagant lifestyle was beyond our means. Cynthia was not filthy rich. She was not even grubbily rich. And neither was I, having devoted many years to a poorly-paid profession. Yet despite this glaring obstacle, we knew there must be some way to avoid winter.

Our first step was to set our sights on the most affordable anti-winterist solution: the permanent move to a heated region.

Living on a nice warm island sounded good.

But islands come in a wide variety of flavours. Together we tried to define exactly what sort of island we were looking for. We decided we wanted a heated island that was hurricane-free, cyclone-free, tornado-free, tidal wave-free, earthquake-free, volcanic-eruption-free, and nuclear bomb-test-free. Somewhere not too big and not too populated. And English-speaking if possible, since neither of us are what you'd call gifted linguists. (Despite years of mandatory French classes I confess to being of the "ex-squeezay moi / toot sweet / au reservoir" school of Canadian bilingualism. And Cynthia's even worse: she thinks of me as suave and educated because of my smooth mastery of "Zee Frawnsh.")

Cynthia and I also wanted to find somewhere with a mellow political scene. Ever since hitting middle age, all the fun seemed to have gone out of riots, rallies, rebellions and revolutions. And we were looking for a place free from tourist trap nightlife. We also wanted an island free from mosquitos and poisonous snakes and people-eating sharks and other dangerous wild beasts. In short, we wanted no scary anything. (Perhaps in my description of myself, "chicken-hearted wussy-pussy" should have been underlined.) And last but by no means least, we needed to find something affordable. Admittedly, it was a tall order.

We began researching all the summery islands of the planet Earth. We sat for three years in Winnipeg's big downtown library. In winter, we sat sweating into our long johns while reading about tropical Pacific islands. On hot summer days we sat inside in the nauseating air conditioning reading thick reference books about spice-scented Caribbean islands. Gradually we eliminated one island after another. In the final result there was one island of great interest to us, although there was hardly any information about it. We took that as a good sign. The kind of place we wanted wouldn't be widely written about.

The island was called St. Helena.

All we could find out about it was the same small paragraph repeated in endless encyclopedias and geography texts. (At that time, the internet was still a new technology and there were no St. Helena websites.) We learned that St. Helena was tiny, just 47 square miles, a British colony, isolated in the South Atlantic Ocean, population about 5,000. No airstrip. Serviced by one ship, the RMS *St. Helena*. Climate: equable. Language: English.

5

Government by Island Council and Crown Appointed British Governor. Death-place of Napoleon Bonaparte, in 1821.

Intrigued, we searched everywhere for more information. At the University of Winnipeg library we found a rare prize: a decaying, brittle, yellowing set of St. Helena Governor's Annual Reports, covering the years 1926 to 1961. From these reports we were able to learn things that we would otherwise have been entirely ignorant of. Things like the price of butter on the island in 1938.

We tried asking well-travelled people about St. Helena, but no one we spoke to had even heard of it. Another good sign.

So we decided to visit St. Helena and see for ourselves. During a six month stay we fell in love with the little-known island in the sun and we decided to live there.

We returned to Canada and worked for another five years. We economized. We sold our car. We bought bicycles and rode them year-round.

Cycling on dark icy roads through snowdrifts at temperatures of forty below zero is not only a budget-conscious form of transportation; it is also a strong motivator to emigrate to a subtropical island. The experience has the effect of reaffirming one's basic anti-winterist beliefs.

On those deathly cold dark bike rides, with the

frozen rock-hard tires slipping and sliding on the ice-lumpy roads – with a relentless head wind slicing and dicing my exposed face like a K-tel Veg-a-matic – I often thought, "I bet this is what Hell is *really* like."

Reports of an Eternal Lake of Fire in Hell are in all likelihood a complete fabrication (since anyone who's ever been to Hell would, of course, be a chronic liar). When you get there, most likely you'll just find endless ice and snow and vicious slicing/dicing winds. Hell probably looks exactly like Manitoba on a cold night in January.

YOU (surprised): "*This* is Hell? Brrrrrrrrrr! Where in hell's the Eternal Lake of Fire?"

DEVIL (enjoying himself): "I've redecorated. Do you like it?"

*   *   *

During those long dreary winters, the bright spot for us was always the arrival, by mail, of the St. Helena newspapers. We had bought a subscription to the weekly news-sheet while we were on the island, and every four months or so a big rolled-up bundle would reach us in Canada. We'd read them in chronological order, savouring each issue. They did more than keep us informed about island events; they kept our island dream alive on the darkest, coldest days.

In one issue Cynthia noticed an unusual item for sale in the classified ads:

A small cottage on 1.9 acres of land situated on the sheltered side of Woody Ridge...

Houses rarely come up for sale on St. Helena, and by St. Helenian law at that time, a property could be sold to an off-islander only after being offered to the local market for a three-month period. By the time we were reading the ad, the three-month period had already passed.

We contacted the owner. The property was still for sale. The house had been sitting empty for over twenty years and lacked all modern conveniences. No electricity. No plumbing. No telephone. Located down a muddy two-rut track. Remarkably, the locals had passed on this dream-home. The price, by subtropical island standards, was very, very reasonable.

We asked for photos and received six fuzzy shots. One grainy picture showed an ancient donkey munching on weeds that were engulfing the crumbling porch. We enquired about him. His name was Patrick. He came with the house.

We didn't hang about. We bought the place, sight unseen. As it turned out, this "impulse buying" actually took almost two years. We went on safari through a jungle of red tape.

And so it came about that on an appropriately bone-chilling day in January, 2001, Cynthia and I boarded a plane at Winnipeg International Airport, bound for London, England. From there we'd head for Cardiff to catch the March 8th sailing of the RMS *St. Helena*, island bound.

As the plane took off we were both nervous. After all the years – *years!* – of searching, planning and struggle, we were actually finally doing it.

And suddenly it seemed crazy.

We were leaving behind family and friends and all that was familiar, to move to a faraway culture where we'd always be foreigners.

I took one long last look out the plane window at the endless flat, white frozen prairie. I needed to ward off the insane feeling that I was already missing Manitoba. Just then I had a comforting thought: we have a lawnmower named Patrick.

I started thinking about St. Helena – our new home. On the globe it's just a solitary flyspeck about midway between South America and Africa – one of the most isolated islands on earth. A country where no airplane has ever landed. A distant outpost, where only one ship makes regular contact with the outside world. We were moving to The Land That Time Forgot. No cell phones. No automatic banking machines. I remembered reading in the island newspaper about the big event on St. Helena in 1997 – *the arrival of television*.

I got to thinking about the people – the "Saints," as

9

they're called – a fascinating mixed-blood race whose forefathers hailed from diverse corners of The British Empire. A friendly blend of East Indian, English, African, Scottish, Chinese and Irish ancestry. Many Saints have never been off the island and have never seen an elevator. Or an escalator. I remembered a woman calling an escalator a "conveyor belt." I thought about the Saints I'd met who've never seen a train or a plane or a shopping mall... or even a traffic light.

It had been almost two hundred years since the island had its brief encounter with world-wide fame. Napoleon Bonaparte had been imprisoned on St. Helena in 1815. After his death on the island in 1821, St. Helena slipped quietly from the minds of most people – a distant, sleepy, forgotten backwater. The happy result is that the island's captivating beauty is almost completely undisturbed.

As might be expected in a place not plagued by "progress" and development, there is an unemployment problem. No one from the "The Big World," as it's called, is permitted to take a job that could be done by a Saint. However, there's no law against creating your own job, so I figured I'd quit my long career as a Professional Ne'er-Do-Well and become an artist or a poet or an author or something.

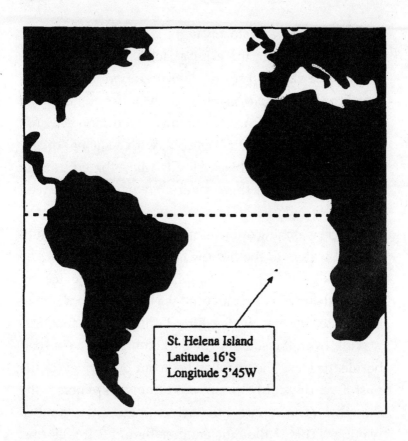

St. Helena Island
Latitude 16'S
Longitude 5'45W

Chapter Three

Salty Dog – A Seaman's Log

It was a dark and stormy night...

No, let's not start there. Let's back up a bit.

It was a dark and stormy late afternoon. The Captain eased the RMS *St. Helena* through the locks of the Queen Alexandra Dock at Cardiff, out toward the dark, heaving, wild sea. The March air was cold, with a slicing/dicing wind, and churning black clouds filled the entire sky.

Even though there were over one hundred passengers and fifty-six crew on board, I was alone on the rear deck, watching our walking-speed progress through the still waters of the narrow cement-walled locks. The max-dosage of anti-nausea pills had left me feeling detached and very stupid, but I was just lucid enough to recognize the man in the little family group that was waving from the solitary car parked on the access road beside the lock. The man had been our bus driver for the past five days. My brain ploddingly assembled the thought: "That's our bus driver... and his family... waving." Then I thought another thought. It was this: "...duh..." Then another: "Wave back." I returned their waving. I felt good about being there on deck to wave. If I hadn't been, their effort to wish us bon voyage would have gone unnoticed.

Our departure had been delayed for five days while engineers worked round-the-clock to repair a cracked piston on one of the massive engines of the RMS *St. Helena*. On the first day of the delay, most of the passengers had reacted to the news with disappointed resignation. But as each day brought another announcement of yet another day's delay, their mood became increasingly foul.

Cynthia and I, on the other hand, were delighted by the delay. We had no schedule to keep and to us it meant a free, floating hotel in Cardiff, with three fancy meals each day and a free movie on board ship each night. The shipping company had been good enough to provide a free shuttle-bus service to downtown Cardiff for shopping trips, and to hire a large bus for tours of the Welsh countryside. They also picked up the tab at museums and art galleries and lunch-stop restaurants. Cynthia and I had just spent the last two months painting and plastering a semi-heated, restoration-still-in-progress Bed and Breakfast in exchange for super-low rent, so we welcomed the unexpected windfall of an all-expenses-paid high-end holiday in Wales.

But very few of the other passengers did. They had plans – plans that were getting all screwed up by the delay. They had hotels booked in Cape Town, and reservations on return flights to the UK. Not to worry, they were told, the ship would still get to Cape Town on time – by cutting down on the time they would have on St. Helena.

And so, for five days, we toured Wales with a busload of increasingly disgruntled elderly tourists who had paid for and expected a winter visit to the subtropical Island of St. Helena, in the beautiful blue South Atlantic Ocean, and instead were visiting the Dylan Thomas Museum in extremely non-subtropical rainy Wales. The resentment of cracked pistons and cracked poets was a palpable presence.

Like paid-to-be-cheerful camp counsellors, the ship's crew tried valiantly to "jolly-along" the marooned-in-port passengers, but their efforts failed. The aged passengers mutated into a form of human being I'd never encountered before: ancient sullen teenagers. They grudgingly joined in the organized jolly fun, full of attitude: "Okay, *okay* already! I'll *do* it! But this *really* sucks."

Revenge was the probable motive, when, on the fourth night of the delay, the crew chose to subject the pouting passengers to a movie called *The Perfect Storm*. It is a depressing tale, supposedly true, about a fishing boat caught in a massive storm in the middle of the Atlantic Ocean, in which everyone drowns. The End. The movie owes its box office success to its extremely realistic special effects portraying just how terrifying the giant waves of an angry ocean are. So we sat in the lounge of a ship with a cracked piston and watched, wondering just when *we* would head way out into the middle of the Atlantic.

Of course we all began wondering if we wanted any part of this going-out-on-the-ocean lark at all. And the next day, with a great big storm brewing, the Captain announced that we would sail on the evening tide.

Now at last we were moving.

Due to the long delay, all well-wishing friends and relatives of the passengers had long since gone home.

I was much too sedated to be scared, but the ominous scene before me unfolded like the beginning of a very heavy movie. As the darkening gloom of the storm closed in over the cold afternoon, the ship crawled slowly along the cement canal, to the mournful accompaniment of crying seagulls and a shrieking wind. We were working our way through the huge deserted and decrepit dockyards, past a row of giant rusted cranes that lined the canal, past mothballed old brick warehouses with broken and dirty windows, past heaps of industrial junk rusting behind rusting chain-link fences, and past one little car with a family of four strangers waving at me; the only witnesses to our departure into the surging black ocean beyond. A more pathetic and dismal bon voyage party could not be imagined.

My brain blipped its sluggish blip: *Wave.* I waved. *Thank you for coming to see us off – very nice of you – glad I was here to wave back to you.*

After a few more minutes we came to the end of the

lock and entered the sea. Immediately the ship rolled and bucked furiously. I held onto the railing and watched Cardiff recede. The street lights were on now and all the lit-up houses and buildings looked warm and safe and secure. What the hell were we doing out here? It didn't seem possible that this was the beginning of a two-week voyage of four-and-a-half-thousand miles to a remote island in the tropics.

I realized I was freezing. My sedated brain eventually arrived at a clever solution to that problem: *go inside.* So I did.

It was a dark and stormy night.

Inside, the corridors were mainly deserted, with just the occasional crew member purposefully striding along from task to task. The passengers were all in their cabins, performing a very strange ritual.

They were "dressing for dinner." This bizarre sea cruising custom involves spending a large part of your holiday dressing up as though you have to go to a life-or-death-important job interview. The object of this carefree holiday fun is to don the most formal, uptight, expensive and uncomfortable clothing that you can come up with, and then to sit at a tilting table in a crazily swaying room enjoying the challenge of attempting to eat food without slopping it all over the clothes. WHEEEEEEE!

The dinner gong sounded over the ship's speakers, but I was feeling a bit queasy. More pills. Soon I was feeling less nauseated but much stupider, which made me want to study the wild party animal in its natural habitat, up close and undetected. So Cynthia and I dressed as uptight as we could and presented ourselves at the dining room.

We met our dinner companions. Introductions were necessary because although we'd spent the last five days at the same happy holiday camp, most people had been too busy sulking to be sociable. The combination of oddly-mixed strangers, uptight clothing, heavy tranquilizers and *Perfect Storm*-induced fear resulted in a superbly weird meal. Then we all retired to our cabins.

The violence of the sea was constantly increasing, as evidenced by the wild tilting and pitching of our little room. I had volunteered to take the upper bunk (not a problem while we were in port, but an entirely different sport in a raging sea). With effort I made it into bed. Soon I wished I hadn't.

It is no accident that doctors never prescribe rolling and tossing near the ceiling of a room as a cure for queasy stomach. The next few hours were devoted to alternating between vomiting and swallowing anti-nausea pills. By holding down each set of pills until the very last possible second, I was able to get enough medication into my bloodstream to become too stupid to register how wretchedly sick I was. Cynthia was sick also, but in a much more middle-of-the-road, easy-listening type of way. I soon abandoned the pointless acrobatics of climbing the seesawing ladder to the upper bunk and just lay on the cabin floor outside the miniature bathroom.

I do not remember slipping into the coma, but I recall being in it. I could hear distant doors banging repeatedly, interspersed with sporadic sound-bites of glass smashing. For a long time I could hear things, but I couldn't move. Eventually though, I recovered the ability to move my limbs and to activate the speech center of my seasick mind. So I asked Cynthia: "Wha... whatime...izzit?" She replied that it was a few minutes past three a.m. Just then we heard a very loud double WHUMP, first on the wall and then on the floor of the cabin next door. This was followed by an enormous SLAM every time the ship rolled downhill sideways. Between us we developed the theory that the elderly woman in the next cabin must have gotten up to use the bathroom, been pitched against the wall and knocked out, and was now lying on the floor, oblivious to the gunshot-type noise her bathroom door was making every time it slammed so violently. Cynthia struck on the good idea of buzzing for the cabin steward, who could look into the situation. She buzzed. We waited. No one came. She buzzed again. Again we waited and again no one came. I volunteered to knock on the woman's door to see if she was all right. I thought I might be able to do it. I certainly had nothing left in my stomach, so my thinking was, what have I got to lose? The only thing really wrong with me was that I was having out-of-body experiences during which I'd wonder why Zontar had ever sent me to a watery planet like this.

Very slowly I kneeled, then stood up. I opened our door and lurched out into the corridor. I knocked and got no answer. I knocked again, this time louder. Still no answer, so I pounded. Nothing. I reported the results to Cynthia. We decided I should go find a cabin steward. So I staggered off, riding the deserted corridors.

There was no one in the steward's pantry nearest our cabin. I careened toward the front of the ship, smashing into walls when they came at me suddenly, and taking a few backward steps whenever the hallway unexpectedly tilted steeply uphill. I arrived at the main lounge without seeing anyone. The big room was deserted. Tables and chairs were tipped over. Magazines from the tables were strewn all over the floor. The magnetic door-catches of the library bookshelves were being overpowered by leaping books. The doors opened and slammed violently as the books hurled themselves to the floor, poltergeist-style. I teetered in the doorway for a few minutes listening to the staccato door slams randomly punctuating the constant drone of the ship's engines.

A magazine on the floor in front of me caught my eye. I read the cover: "Dylan At Sixty."

Wow. Dylan? At *sixty?* Wow!

hmmm…

Once upon a time you looked so fine
you were in yer prime, had lotsa time
did'n yooo?
time for beers an' lookin' in mirrors
but now it appears all-the-time the years were
kid'n yooo

You used to laugh about
everybody that was hangin' out
but now ya don't look so slim
now ya wag a double chin
as you Polident yer dentures to eat
yer next meeeeeeal

How does it *feel*?
How does it feel?
to be an old *crone*?
need die-rections *home*
like a fuse that's *blown*
like a toothless comb...

I pondered all this for a while, and then remembered what I was supposed to be doing. I decided to try a different deck level. Negotiating the stairs on my hands and knees, I eventually reached the other eerily deserted furniture-strewn lounge at the rear of the ship. By now I had covered a large area of the RMS *St. Helena* and had seen absolutely no one. I paused for a moment of panic and paranoia: had everyone abandoned ship? Had we missed it because of the coma? I gathered a thought together: keep looking.

As I stumbled past another unoccupied steward's pantry, dishes smashed to the floor. The wild dancing of the ship was beginning to creep up on me, and I knew I was going to be sick again. I wondered who the Einstein was that said matter cannot be created or destroyed. Probably some prissy pampered landlubber who never retched his stomach dry only to have it magically fill up with barf again. WHAT GOOD ARE LAWS OF PHYSICS IF NO-ONE'S GOING TO ENFORCE THEM?

I knew I must abandon my mission and return to the bathroom in our cabin. On the way there, strange memories passed through my head. I remembered being a young boy, sitting in the outhouse (or "biffy" as we called it) at the summer cottage, reading a Bugs Bunny comic book. I always took reading material to the biffy with me, as a means of avoiding the interior decor. My mother had decided that we children could painlessly learn our multiplication tables during the summer holidays if she wallpapered the biffy walls with the times tables. This of course was a direct violation of the Geneva Convention, which clearly states that children should not have to endure such mind-numbing filth while on holiday, and should instead engage in higher intellectual pursuits, such as reading Bugs Bunny comics.

So as I reeled along the pitching passageways of the RMS *St. Helena*, somewhere in the North Atlantic, I recalled being in the biffy at Gull Lake, Manitoba, Canada, and reading an episode involving Bugs and Yosemite Sam (pronounced "Yo-*sem*-it-tee," but at the time I pronounced it "*Yo*-sem-mite"). Bugs and Sam were going after buried treasure on a distant treasure island. They bought a boat, but had a disagreement over what to name it. Bugs wanted to call it "The Nautilus," but Sam wanted "Sea Queen," so they compromised and called it the "Nau-Sea."

I reflected briefly on how much more Bugs had taught me about real life than "nine times eight equals ninety-eight" ever did.

I reached our cabin and its bathroom just in time. I hadn't seen anyone anywhere on the ship. The door in the next cabin was still slamming loudly on its erratic schedule. When I emerged from the bathroom I lay on the floor and explained that my travels had produced no results. I pictured the frail old woman in the next cabin being rolled back and forth across the cabin floor in an ever-expanding pool of blood emanating from a large gash in her unconscious head.

"I guess we'll just let her die... if she's still on board," I thought. Then I blacked out.

The morning brought with it a miracle. The sun was shining brightly through the cabin window and the room had a much better idea of the correct position for a room to be in (walls vertical, floor and ceiling horizontal).

Like the poet said, "Job Number One is to dumb the thing down," so I took some more pills. When my stupidity level was properly adjusted, Cynthia and I ventured out of the cabin.

Another miracle: there were people on the ship.

We went to the dining room. A handful of passengers were scattered around the room, nibbling gingerly on dry toast. Only a couple of dining room staff were present. A chat with them revealed that almost everyone on board – including the crew and the ship's doctor – had been sick all night. No one was feeling particularly bushy-tailed just at the moment. We nibbled and returned to our cabin. Just as we were going in, the woman next door emerged from her cabin. She smiled weakly. No head-gash. Alive.

Gradually we all recovered, and in a couple of days the atmosphere on board was on the upswing. The weather was getting warmer each day as we ploughed ever southward. Soon life began to resemble the travel brochures: lazy hours in the deck chairs beside the little swimming pool, hot sun, brilliant blue sky, flying fish and dolphins leaping from the tropical blue-green water, fantastic gourmet meals, and zillions of stars in the sky at night.

The ordeal was over and the memory of it was fading. Fear was being replaced by anticipation as we, like Bugs and Sam, neared our treasure island. Soon we would reach St. Helena, "The Jewel Of The South Atlantic."

Chapter Four

The Amazing Nature-ini

No matter how much you've been anticipating arriving at St. Helena, the actual sight of it comes as a delightful shock.

After so many days of staring at an unbroken brilliant blue emptiness that stretches to the horizon in every direction, the traveller en route to St. Helena gradually gets subconsciously duped into believing that the South Atlantic Ocean is infinite. And then one day – there it is! Gigantic sheer walls of rock rising way up high out of the crashing waves.

There is one word that best describes the sight of this towering land that stands alone, far, far out in the big huge sea. St. Helena looks *majestic*.

After all those days of seeing nothing at all but water, it's hard to adjust to the idea that you're seeing something that *isn't* water. And it's also hard to believe that a sight so beautiful is really real. The solitary island sits mounted on the ocean's horizon, looking very imposing, but at the same time, mirage-like.

To experience this surreal reality is to experience one of Nature's very best magic tricks. Setting up this trick took millions of years. First it took unknown millions to get the island to appear above sea level. Then around fourteen million years went into fine tuning (seven for further volcanic activity and about another seven for cooling and sculpture by erosion). St. Helena Island represents the tip of a huge volcanic cone.

"An emerald set in bronze" is an often quoted, perfect description of St. Helena. The phrase poetically and concisely describes the fact that the higher interior regions are green and lush whereas the coastal areas are barren, treeless yellow/brown rock, often nature-carved into giant weird and wonderful sculptures. The rolling interior highlands, where every shade of green meets the eye, are reminiscent of Ireland, while strange, stark, boulder-strewn coastal areas bring to mind the surface of the moon.

Deep valleys and winding ravines cut through towering ranges of peaks. The varying altitude and irregular terrain create a variety of microclimates that support a huge diversity of plant life. During five hundred years of human habitation, plants have been brought to St. Helena from all over the world. For example, Captain Bligh brought ten breadfruit trees to St. Helena in 1792. Often these botanical imports have thrived with a vigour unknown in the lands of their origin.

So a walker on St. Helena is met with an enchanting surrealism: a road or path may be winding through a dense stand of big pines, with the sloping landscape doing a convincing impersonation of a British Columbia

Rain Forest; but just around the next curve the pines have vanished, and a bamboo jungle has appeared.

High up on the damp peaks, mist momentarily erases, then shades in a ghostly soft outline of the prehistoric-looking tree ferns. Here in The Land That Time Forgot, the appearance of a pterodactyl or a brontosaurus would seem absolutely normal.

When hiking in the cool, green, misty highlands, it's hard to believe that this is the same tiny island where cacti bloom in the hot outlying, desert-like badlands.

Magic.

Some place names of interest on St. Helena

The Gates of Chaos, Fairyland, Gorilla's Head, Cow Path, Button Up Corner, Cuckold's Point, Two Gun Saddle, Cathole, Ladies Bath Spring, Goldmine Gate, Fox's Folly, Holdfast Tom, Old Woman's Valley, Old Man's Head, Goat Pound Ridge, The Asses Ears, Shepherd's Hole, Donkey Plain, King and Queen Rocks, Ladies Chair, Alarm Forest, The Haystack, Bonfire Ridge, Iron Pot, Turk's Cap, Bloody Bridge, Repulse Point, Ball Alley, Devil's Punchbowl, Wild Ram Hill, Frightus Rock, Lazy Point, The Dungeon, Nymph's Cottage, Blarney Bridge, Breakneck Valley, Heart Shaped Waterfall.

Chapter Five

Barefoot Cottage
Episode One: Gloom with a View

We were standing in dense undergrowth that was crotch-high. Unfortunately, but not surprisingly, the old donkey, Patrick, had died some time before our arrival on the island. In the absence of his lawn-mowing talents, the jungle, like bad taste in music, was slowly but surely taking over.

The previous owner had very generously offered to drive us up to the place, to show us around and to hand over the keys. Even though the purchase was long since a done deal, his manner, while friendly enough, was somewhat cautious. A bit wary. As if at any minute he expected us to go berserk. I think he was afraid that we'd think he had sold us a house of horrors. He needn't have worried on my account though. I was a satisfied customer.

Our house of horrors was situated in the prettiest scenery I'd ever seen anywhere. A huge green gently rolling hill, dotted with grazing cows, provided the idyllic foreground. To the left of this big green pasture we overlooked the convergence of two green valleys and on the other side of the far valley, peeking out from tall evergreens, was St. Helena's most famous landmark – Napoleon's house. Rising up high behind it was Flagstaff, a conical peak that looks just like every child's drawing of a mountain. Next to Flagstaff was The Barn, a long, flat-topped, wrinkled, bare-rock mountain – site of the original volcano that formed the island (and obligingly extinct for the last seven and a half million years). To our right we could see the yellow-brown desert-like coastal plateau – Prosperous Bay Plain. And forming a stunning background to it all, the too-blue-to-be-true South Atlantic Ocean.

To my way of thinking, when you've got a view like that, a house of horrors is a minor snafu. Unfortunately, Cynthia was having an attack of reality.

For me, looking at the view banished the heebie-jeebies I got whenever I looked around inside the house. But Cynthia's heebie-jeebies were of a higher voltage. They produced in her a profound state of shock. She could not be resuscitated by scenery.

And I guess that's not really surprising. She has a phobia about spiders.

Our tour guide had opened the door. The three of us had stepped in. The dominant feature of the décor was the bold spider motif. Spiders everywhere. All sizes and speeds. Some just sat in vast webs, motionless and menacing, while a great many others scuttled rapidly past each other on every surface like rush hour at Grand Central Station. Some (and this amazed and revolted even me) could actually *hop* large distances.

I suppose the dirt was the thing I noticed next. I have

lived in degenerate three-bachelor households, where cleaning anything was seen as a sign of weakness, and still, this was something entirely new to me. A quarter of a century is a long time to go between dustings.

I had also never seen termites before that day. I learned that they were the creatures who had built the many stalagmites of dirt on the floor, extending four feet up the walls, all the way around each room. I lifted up a curling corner of the linoleum. Billions and billions of white termites jostled frantically. They looked like high-speed maggots. I could say I'd never seen anything like it, but I had; I'd watched agitated bacteria through a microscope.

Looking mournfully out at us from a dozen framed photos on the walls were The Royal Family. They didn't look too happy. Their faces were discoloured and wrinkled with water stains. The Queen had a ZZ Top beard of mould. Termites had eaten holes in Prince Philip's head and had eerily removed Prince Charles' eyes. Princess Anne's head had been replaced by a large stationary spider.

Black mould coated the inside of the rusting corrugated iron roof. Drips of condensation on the inside of the roof had formed into rivulets, which then ran down the walls. So on the walls, the upward-growing termites' dirt stalagmites were met with downward-growing mould/dirt/congealed slime stalactites. At times I had to relieve the heebie-jeebies by staring through the holes in the roof at the clean, pleasant blue sky.

Our guide opened a small crumbling cupboard door. Inside, another jam-packed swarm of termites battled for space with another horde of spiders.

"Oh dear... termites. That happens when no one's living in a place and I haven't come up here very much... since Patrick died," he said apologetically.

I was raised Canadian; I knew what to say in circumstances like these.

"No problem," I said.

Cynthia was eerily silent.

Patrick and Barefoot Cottage

Barefoot Cottage
Episode two: A Pail Imitation of Luxury

I was hand-washing my seventh filthy sock when I saw what time it was: it was time to build a washing machine. We had cleverly done our laundry on the ship just before we reached the island, but house-cleaning Barefoot Cottage was dirty work and soon we needed to clean our clothes. Actually, "house-cleaning" can't possibly be the right word for getting rid of what accumulates in a house with large holes in the roof that's been abandoned for a quarter of a century. Maybe the correct word is "dis-scuzzing." Yes. We were dis-scuzzing a disgusting mess, and our clothes were, to be polite, soiled.

But I had an immediate aversion to washing clothes by hand, one item at a time. It requires a patience I do not possess. So we built Old Faceful. We based it on a drawing in a book that we'd seen in the Winnipeg Library. The book was called *Pedal Power*. The idea is a bicycle-powered washing machine, which, when pedalled, makes a toilet-plunger go up and down in a pail filled with soapy water and dirty clothes. It was obvious to us that we'd have plenty of dirty clothes in the foreseeable future, so we altered the design to include two pails – a "twin-tubs" model. We built it. And not only does it work, it works well.

We put drains and taps on the bottoms of the two plastic pails. Ten minutes of pedalling with soapy water for the wash "cycle." Then drain and refill with fresh water. Five minutes pedalling for a rinse "cycle." Then simply repeat the rinse "cycle" once more and your whites are whiter and your brights are brighter. For a more user-friendly performance, we added slotted pail-lids, so now the water actually stays *inside* Old Faceful.

But these days I'm thinking, two pails good – four pails better; and I've already worked out the most difficult and important aspect of the new design: the stupid catchy name. I shall call it "The Four Barrel *Garb-erator.*"

Barefoot Cottage
Episode Three: Gruelling Lessons in the School of Cool

I wouldn't say we *worship* our fridge. Worship isn't the right word. Is there a word that means the same as worship, but is just one shade weaker? I looked up *revere* – "to honour and admire profoundly." Close, but not quite strong enough. Somewhere between revere and worship is how we feel about our fridge.

I'm pretty sure you won't find many people who have these feelings for their fridge. Lots of people just take their fridge for granted. I know. I used to be among them. But in life, the more of yourself you put into something, the more satisfaction you get out of it. And Cynthia and I have given freely of ourselves as regards refrigeration.

Without a doubt, it has all been worth it. Refrigerationally speaking, *we have arrived*. Our present-day fridge is our third fridge since moving to the island. The first one we made ourselves and the other two we restored.

Our current appliance is a paraffin powered, gleaming white, full size, ice-cube-producing Electrolux. We found it after searching for over a year. It is one of only two paraffin powered fridges known to exist on the island today. Nowadays most fridges here are electric (useless to those of us without electricity). We were thrilled to find this rare, 1970's vintage, functioning antique. We lovingly restored the rust patches, painted the rusty shelf grills, and siliconed over the gaps in the door-sealing gasket.

We mid-revere/worship it.

It's a giant leap forward from our second fridge, which was a giant leap forward from our first fridge.

Our second fridge was a butane-powered wreck from a wrecked camper van. Inside it was slightly bigger than a shoebox. Almost as big as a Canadian-winter-boots-box. It had a miniature ice cube tray for making miniature ice cubes. But I think the tray was there just as a cruel decoration. It certainly never made any ice cubes. I went so far as to dress the little fridge in a four-inch-thick styrofoam jacket to get it to be cool, but any cooling effect was perceptible only to a highly-trained optimist. It ran off a three-foot-tall steel gas cylinder, which, when sitting on the kitchen floor, marred the country-kitchen style décor that we were going for. The steel cylinder gave the country-kitchen a disturbing and demented industrial feel. As if you were planning on doing a bit of arc welding while the apple pie bakes.

But the décor didn't suffer for long. We found out that there was an explosion danger associated with having the cylinder indoors. The cylinder had to go outdoors and be connected to the fridge with a length of hose. This meant we needed a hole in the kitchen wall to run the hose through.

Fortunately for us though, I am leading a charmed life. On the day we moved in, I found a rusty brace-and-bit hand drill lying on the kitchen floor beside a dead rat. With the drill, it took us only a few days to hand-drill through the six-inch concrete wall. It took only a few more days for the big blisters on my hands to heal, but by that time the fridge had flickered, fizzled and died forever – bringing about a return to the bad old days. The days when we first moved into Barefoot Cottage and had no fridge.

Finding yourself fridgeless is quite disorienting. I was surprised to find it more disorienting than waking up in a dark room and feeling the walls for non-existent light switches. Picture this: Baking subtropical heat. Sunstroked, sweaty, light-headed and dying of thirst, you stumble to the kitchen to get a cold drink. Once there, you stand – immobilized and confused – until your cooked mind whispers softly to you, "There *is* no fridge."

We had considered digging a root cellar. "Root cellar" is a high tech term for "hole in the ground." This primitive method of refrigeration was known to us because it was common among early pioneers on the Canadian Prairie. But no one on St. Helena had one, possibly because of the rats, so we went back to thinking.

I should mention that when we moved into Barefoot Cottage there already was a "kitchen appliance" (if we use the term loosely enough) for keeping butter and fish and so on. This appliance is known locally as a "safe." It's a box up on legs. The box part is a wooden frame covered with window screen, or "wire-gauze" in Saint-speak. The wire-gauze box has a door and a couple of shelves inside. When you put your food inside "the safe," it's safe from flies.

I looked at this strange device and thought about its design-logic. It revealed a remarkable parallel between the Saints and the English: a sort of frugal minimalism. The Saints do not put screens on their windows. As a result, sometimes there are flies in the houses. But no problem – the butter and the fish are safe in their little wire-gauze box. Meanwhile, back at The Mother Country, the English do not heat their houses. As a result, their houses are deathly cold. But no problem – the teapot's snuggled in its little quilted coat and the boiled egg's cozy in its little knitted hat. There may be a future for someone selling shoes to the Saints and the English. Shoes for those who have no carpeting in their homes. Shoes with carpet samples glued onto the bottoms.

Anyway, we found the safe interesting, but it did nothing about keeping milk from going sour. The other tiny drawback to the safe in Barefoot Cottage was that it was infested (or "festered" in Saint-speak) with termites.

Here, I digress, to mention that a hibiscus bush behind our house was half-eaten by termites. The situation was pointed out to us in Saint-speak as follows:

"You high-biscuit yonder do be festered."

So the festered safe had to be burned. When this was done Cynthia and I put our heads together and came up with "Mach One" – or should I say "Mock One" – our first fridge. Although it worked, we soon perceived that perhaps there was room for improvement.

It was made of a black plastic garbage can that we filled with ice. Then we wrapped all our Canadian winter clothes around the garbage can and tied them on with belts and ropes. Fortunately, having left Winnipeg in January, we had an ample supply of eiderdown parkas, puffy vests and heavy sweaters to use as fridge insulation.

You may be wondering where we got the ice. This is where our fridge design begins to show a distinct lack of "set-it-and-forget-it" convenience. Each Monday, Wednesday and Friday the fish truck tours round the island selling the locally caught tuna, wahoo, mackerel and bullseye. It announces its arrival with a merry toot of its horn which plays the theme from *The Lone Ranger*, or as snobs say, "The William Tell Overture" – dahling. You know the tune: the one that answers the musical question "Where does The Lone Ranger take his garbage?" (ta-da *dump*, ta-da *dump*, ta-da *dump dump dump*). Three days a week, while I struggled on with home renovations – just decorative stuff like a roof – Cynthia hiked up the steep two-rut road to the old disused flax mill, to wait for the fish truck. She took along three big plastic pails and when the truck arrived, she'd buy three pails of ice – if there was any for sale, which was not always the case. Then she'd haul the three pails home, using a back and forth relay method. Getting the ice could be anything from a one-hour to a three-hour job, depending on the fish truck's schedule, which varies with the number of roadside customers the driver encounters and how long each one gabs, which varies with the juiciness of the news and rumours on any given day.

Once we had the ice it was a simple matter of undoing all the coats and sweaters embundling the "fridge," fishing out the food and drinks from the smelly fish-water in the garbage can, dumping out the reeking water, adding new fish-scented ice, replacing the food and drinks, and re-embundling the garbage can with the coats, sweaters, belts and ropes. The disembundling and re-embundling had to be gone through every time anyone wanted something from the fridge.

During a moment of revulsion, as I inhaled the stench of old fish while fumbling for a slippery juice bottle that was bobbing in the slime, I recalled the fridge at my rich aunt's house.

My family had visited her at her elegant home in Ontario on our way to The World's Fair in Montreal in 1967. The fridge she had was a model I'd seen advertised on TV, but she was the only person I knew that actually owned one. It was a Hovercraft-type model, in which you plugged a hose from your vacuum cleaner into the bottom of the fridge, turned on the vacuum, and your fridge floated on a cushion of air. In the TV ad, a smug, manicured, stewardess-like housewife effortlessly pushed the fridge across the kitchen with one finger, and then smilingly squeegie-mopped the already-sparkling floor where the fridge had sat. I begged my aunt for a demonstration and she kindly obliged. She floated her fridge magically around the kitchen – JUST LIKE ON TV!

...But the sharp stench of sour fish snapped me back from my reverie. Suddenly I loathed our cruddy living conditions. As I put the lid back on the "fridge" I gave myself a stern talking to:

"Cynthia deserves better than this! You've *got* to come up with a better fridge! Think Rex! *Think!* How can you get this fish-stinking garbage can to float around the kitchen?"

Barefoot Cottage
Episode Four: Too Bad I Had to Use the "S" Word

Cynthia had a faraway look in her eyes. She was obviously lost in thought. Suddenly she asked me, "How long have we been living here now?"

My answer was swift and knowledgeable: "Four outhouse holes."

I have learned that the outhouse hole provides a reliable unit of time measurement. But it differs somewhat from the Rolex watch in that it periodically requires the owner to dig a new nine-foot hole and move a smelly building. Also, an outhouse owner will soon notice a difference in status between being an outhouse owner and being a Rolex watch owner. No one is ever going to gush "Oooh! Is that a *real* outhouse? Wow! I am *so* impressed!"

But I thought I'd found a way to significantly decrease the status-gap... for I thought I'd found a way to eliminate the dig-and-move inconvenience of the toilet-chronometer. I had been reading a book called *A Parrot In The Pepper Tree* by Chris Stewart. It's the true story of an Englishman who leaves behind his career as a musician and struggles to establish a life for himself and his family on a remote sheep farm in the mountains of Spain. On page 66 I read the following passage:

"Now, the chumbo (or more properly chumbera) is a prickly pear, a plant that adorns almost every cortijo in the peninsula. In the sixteenth century, when it was brought back along with agaves and gold and silver from the Americas, it was discovered not only to have tasty fruit but to have the extraordinary property of absorbing shit."

Those last few words echoed over and over again inside my head, until I began to think I was a character in a bad late movie:

...the extraordinary property of absorbing shit
...the extraordinary property of absorbing shit
...the extraordinary property of absorbing shit
EUREKA!

Absorbing shit! What a tantalizing revolutionary advance! What a quantum leap! Could it be? Just toss a few prickly pear plants down the hole and *you never have to dig or move again?* And St. Helena is *rich* in prickly pear! *Oh Rolex-flaunting Yuppies, eat your hearts out!*

I carefully read and re-read the passage, but the actual "how-to" became no clearer to me. What I needed was more information. So I immediately fired off a letter to the author.

Incidentally, I had intended to avoid using the word "shit" in my book, thus giving it the distinction of being the only book published in the last twenty-five years devoid of the word. But Chris Stewart had, of course, used the word "shit" in his book, so I reluctantly decided to write to him using the technical terminology with which he was familiar. I have had a horror of seeing the word "shit" in print ever since my disturbing encounter with a feral mum and her unfortunate toddler in a Winnipeg shopping mall. The obese, missing-link-like feral mum was attired in an elegant tent-sized bright pink sweatshirt. Two words were emblazoned in billboard-size black letters across her spacious chest. Her child, at the just-learning-to-read stage, was staring intently at the letters, trying to sound out and understand the important words that mummy so badly wanted all the world to know: "SHIT HAPPENS." Sadly, I was not wearing a "WHAT THE HELL'S THE MATTER WITH PEOPLE?" sweatshirt that day.

Anyway, I wincingly wrote to the author about "shit" absorption.

January 3, 2003

Dear Mr. Stewart,

...or may I just call you "Chris"? I think you might agree that a first-name basis is best when discussing a down-home subject of a somewhat personal nature... so I'll just call you "Chris" and you can call me "Rex", OK?

Chris, I'm writing to plumb the depths of your knowledge on the fascinating subject of the shit-absorbing property of the "chumbo" or "chumbera" or "prickly pear" plant.

I have read your rather brief dissertation on the prickly pear's "extraordinary property of absorbing shit" in your book A PARROT IN THE PEPPER TREE. Chris, I enjoyed your book very much, but if you don't mind my saying so, I think you could have gone into greater detail about the plant's shit-absorbing property... but of course, that's just my opinion, and I suppose you can't please all of the people all of the time. Perhaps you had long heated arguments with your editors and publishers about it... perhaps you wanted to expand the shit-absorbing section of your book and they didn't want you to, thinking some readers might regard it as being in bad taste. I have no way of knowing how it came about that this topic got such short shrift in your book.

Chris, by now you may be getting worried that this letter may be from an unbalanced individual with a decidedly unhealthy fascination with the subject of shit absorption.

I assure you that you couldn't be more wrong.

I am a balanced person with a practical, rational and healthy interest in this topic.

Allow me to explain: Two years ago, having exited my career as a professional musician, my wife and I sold our house in Canada and bought a remote, overgrown two acre farm and derelict three room house - (no electricity, no phone, no plumbing, partial roof) - on the isolated tiny island of St. Helena, in the South Atlantic Ocean - about midway between

South America and Africa - (no airstrip, one ship). We based our decision to buy this place on the strength of six photos. No one had lived here for about twenty-five years, and our first jobs upon moving in were to remove the dead rat from the kitchen and to burn the furniture, which was crawling with zillions of termites. We have cleared land and attempted to establish a small coffee plantation, although the two sheep that we bought to mow the grass between the coffee trees have chosen instead to eat the coffee trees.

Alert friends noticed some similarities between our situation and yours and sent us DRIVING OVER LEMONS and later, A PARROT IN THE PEPPER TREE.

Naturally, we read of your family's travails with more than a casual interest.

As I've said Chris, we have no plumbing; we have an outhouse; and, needless to say, we have shit; and St.Helena has a wealth of prickly pear plants.

So now, to my question: how exactly are these two types of matter combined for the benefit of humankind?

If you would be so kind as to furnish whatever details you may have, I would be very much obliged. I enclose a stamp and a self-addressed envelope in hopes of hearing from you on this urgent and important matter.

Yours truly,
Rex Bartlett

It was very nice of Mr. Stewart to take the time and trouble to reply to my letter, and within a couple of outhouse holes we had deciphered his tiny handwriting.

April 8th

Dear Rex

Sorry to have taken so long to reply to your letter, ... I hope you have in the meantime established an interim solution to your delicate problem ... or perhaps you have gone under? Anyway, to be truthful, my knowledge of the subject in question is pretty slim; it's just a phenomenon that I have observed in my wanderings around the area. In the countryside nobody has — or had, as Crapper's patent water-closet has colonised even the remotest spots now — either drainage or a lavatory. There are always Chimbos around the house, and the chimbo is the place where the family would traditionally go for a crap. There is never any evidence of this activity in the surroundings of the farms, even when there are big families involved. Somebody once told me "the Chimbo is a great eater of shit." And so I drew the conclusion I wrote in my book. I think the truth lies somewhere between the sun and the wind and the rain and the pigs and the dogs. I wish you the very best of luck with your idyll; it sounds wonderful.

Best wishes

For those who don't have a magnifying glass handy or the time to decode the calligraphy, the gist of it can be gathered from a couple of lines: "...*to be truthful, my knowledge of the subject in question is pretty slim... Somebody once told me 'the Chumbo is a great eater of shit.'*"

So after receiving his letter, I was no closer to living a one-outhouse-hole life. But I always admire an honest man. And the letter was by no means completely lacking in wisdom, for Chris Stewart has penned a beautiful Zen-like philosophy that applies universally, even though he was writing in reference to shit and shit-absorption. I quote: "*I think the truth lies somewhere between the sun and the wind and the rain and the pigs and the dogs.*" Next time I'm out there Seeking The Truth, I'm going to try to remember that – and it would make such a classy sweatshirt.

Barefoot Cottage
Episode Five:
What Man Hath Joined Together,
Let No God Tear Asunder

When we first moved into Barefoot Cottage it was hard to say if it was a two-room or a three-room house. The "not-the-kitchen" room was subdivided by a masonite partition, thereby sort of creating two rooms from one, sort of totaling three. I say "sort of" because the partition wasn't a proper wall. It didn't reach all the way up to the roof. Interior decorators would probably refer to walls like this as being in the "Public Toilet Cubicle Style." Real estate agents would of course want to sanitize this and make it sound desirable, like this:

Kitchen plus PTC-style living rm./bed rm.

Happily, there are no real estate agents on St. Helena.

I'm not big on having public toilet ambiance in the bedroom, and besides, the wall was festered, so we tore it down and burned it.

Since then we've added on a tool shed to the back of the house, raising Barefoot Cottage to genuine full-on three-room status. I found the building process vastly educational. Due to termite-festering, the building materials of choice here are concrete and corrugated iron. I learned that concrete is made up of cement, gravel, sand and water. Here on St. Helena, the cement is imported in hernia-making surreal fifty kilogram bags. The gravel is produced locally by crushing rock, and the sand is pumped up from the bottom of the sea, near the wharf in Jamestown.

Here, a bag of cement will soon harden into a useless lump because of the damp subtropical air. So it's important not to order your cement until you have your gravel and sand in place, ready to use.

I learned that there can be the odd snafu when getting gravel. For example, there may not be any. You'll also need a truck and the truck may be broken, requiring the replacement of any number of the ten million parts of a truck. Parts must come from England or Africa and the delay might be measured in weeks, months, or outhouse-holes.

Although it's rare, at times there's a specific alignment of the planets that produces a mysterious synchronicity of cosmic forces. This results in the simultaneous existence of both gravel *and* a functioning truck on St. Helena. But even then, things can still fizzle, due to *a previously unforeseen obstacle*. My personal favourite obstacle in this category is "The Driver Doesn't Work Tuesdays."

I learned that getting sand presents an even greater challenge than getting gravel, because we must add more variables. It goes like this: "The sea's too rough to pump sand." Followed by "The pump's broken." Followed by "The truck's broken." Followed by "The driver doesn't work Tuesdays." And by Wednesday of course, "The sea's too rough to pump sand." But for those with a will of iron, the day will eventually dawn when you actually possess both gravel and sand. Then it's time to stride boldly on to the next step – discovering that there's no cement on the island.

You don't mind. By now you know all about how to wait. And when the cement arrives on the island you will gamely re-enter the labyrinthine struggle to secure both a functioning truck and a driver, because the distant promise of the thrill of victory is an irresistible lure. Your pile of gravel and your pile of sand reassure you. They speak to you of your superhuman endurance. They are the omen and they are the sign. From them you glory in the certain knowledge that someday – maybe not tomorrow, maybe not next week, maybe not even this year, but someday – *someday you shall build.*

Constructing our tool shed has changed me.

The island's man-made structures now have new meaning for me. I am filled with awe as I behold the miracle of a single car garage rising majestically from the landscape, far more impossible and baffling than The Pyramids or Stonehenge. I can only stare, mystified and humbled, and wonder, "How did that ever get there?"

Chapter Six

My Fly Spot

St. Helena is a make-your-own-fun kind of place and the Saints are quite keen on sports. Cricket, soccer (which they call football), skittles and rifle shooting are all popular.

Personally, I have always been bored by organized sports. They lack suspense. Someone will win and someone will lose. Who and by how much is, to me, just pointless trivia. Needless to say, this attitude has caused me to be an outcast all my life. As could be expected, my heterosexual orientation was called into question whenever I failed to be excited by men-only activities that involve getting sweaty and patting each other on the bum and orgasmically hugging each other when someone "scores."

But we are all born to be who we are, and I have meandered through life blissfully ignorant of the intense and unnecessary challenges going on around me on the playing field.

So, in my ignorance, on St. Helena I mistook the structures I saw in the front yards of some of the country houses for some kind of sport-related equipment. They looked like smallish football or soccer goal posts, and I assumed they were there for practice. Eventually I learned that these "goal posts" are actually there for hanging up a pig by its hind legs and slitting its throat. To the best of my knowledge this is done in a purely practical frame of mind and there are no throat-slitting championships held here at all.

I must say that male Saints have not been as alarmed by my sportlessness as Canadian men were. Perhaps Saints mistakenly assume that sportlessness is normal for Canadian men, and therefore do not view it as a disturbing personal defect in my character.

My one and only close encounter of the sporting kind has proved useless as a basis for male-bonding jock-talk with the local guys. I have experienced "curling," but since it requires a long sheet of ice it is completely unheard-of on subtropical St. Helena.

It was during one very long Canadian winter that my calling as a Professional Ne'er-Do-Well led me to pose as an Ice-maker's Assistant at a curling rink in a small prairie town. Although curling is essentially a game of shuffleboard on ice, in Canada it is considered to be a "sport." This particular sport attracts an unusual breed of athlete. For the most part, the ones I encountered had red eyes and red noses. They tended to have huge bellies. They smelled of beer and hard liquor and most of these athletes chain-smoked.

At my job I soon learned of the only pastime more boring than curling. It is *watching* curling. Take a tip: If you're going to watch curling at all, treat yourself to a lobotomy first.

Happily for me, Brian, the Icemaker, also experienced a sensation of brain-death if he watched the graceful athletes perform the breath-taking ballet that is curling. So, after preparing the ice, during games, we'd ignore the curling and chat instead.

Curlin'-n-drinkin' was the main event in town and our services were required twelve hours a day, seven days a week. By the end of that long, long winter we had discussed an extremely wide variety of topics in great detail.

Brian had grown up poor in the slums of a city in Scotland. His family had immigrated to Canada when he was a teenager. I sensed that he may have been scarred forever by the poverty of his childhood:

"None of us could afford a pet... so my friends and I, we'd catch a fly in our hands and put the fly in an icebox. The fly would get colder and colder. We'd check on his condition every few minutes. When he stopped moving altogether we'd take him out and attach a piece of thread to his belly with a drop of wax from a candle. Then we'd tie the other end of the thread to one of our belt loops. The fly would eventually thaw out and fly around in circles on his leash.... Every schoolboy had a pet fly attached to his pants where I lived."

My Fly Spot

See Spot fly.

Fly Spot. Fly!

Buzz, buzz, buzz!

Young Brian's Essay

Chapter Seven

Step Right Up

"Parade Square" in Jamestown – *the* town on St. Helena. It sounds very grand.

When you hear "Parade Square" you probably picture an enormous echoey plaza like you might find in European cities, where flocks of pigeons gawk at flocks of tourists who gawk at the square because they're so amazed to find such a huge open space in such a cramped city. But most strip-mall parking lots in The Big World dwarf Jamestown's Parade Square.

The square is bordered in part by the green and serene Botanical Gardens – home of Anne's Place outdoor café, where you can usually meet an interesting international assortment of friendly sea-farin' yachties while enjoying delicious St. Helena fishcakes. Also facing onto Parade Square are beautiful old buildings: a lovingly-restored church – St. James' – the oldest Anglican church in the Southern Hemisphere; the small, high-ceilinged library that radiates strong colonial outpost vibes and is the oldest public library in the Southern Hemisphere; the old whitewashed courthouse and the little police station, with ancient cannons out front adding to the inescapable feeling of colonial time-warp; the tiny jail; and the bougainvillea-draped arch into "The Castle," where the island's government is headquartered.

But if you're seeing small, quaint, bustling Parade Square for the first time, you probably won't notice any of this. You'll be much too busy being amazed. And awed. Because when standing in Parade Square, Jamestown, St. Helena, you are standing at the foot of Jacob's Ladder.

Six hundred and ninety-nine steps.

Yep. You read right. Six hundred and ninety-nine. Almost straight up.

I've done a few calculations on this and here's what I've come up with: In architecture, ten feet up is generally considered to be a storey. Jacob's Ladder's steps are on average, ten inches high. What this means is that The Ladder is a fifty-eight storey staircase. Now, if a fifty-eight storey outdoor staircase was located among fifty-eight storey skyscrapers, it would be an impressive sight. But when a fifty-eight storey outdoor staircase is located in a country where no building is more than three stories high, you *really* notice it, and trust me, you're *really* impressed.

The scale of the thing takes me back to childhood, to a time when most things were huge. I look at The Ladder, and a voice from my childhood – the voice of CBC TV's *The Friendly Giant* – automatically echoes through my mind: "Look up. Look waaaaay up."

Jamestown's Jacob's Ladder is a structure with the unusual ability to immediately separate all who see it into two distinct groups: those who think, "No way. Not me –

ever," and those who (boldly) think, "Piece-a-cake."

Cynthia and I were, of course, in this second "bold" or "idiotic" group. (I have come to realize, too late in life for it to do me any good, that "bold" and "idiotic" are often interchangeable words.) We, like all members of this second group, reasoned that climbing Jacob's Ladder is, after all, just walking up stairs – a thing we'd already done many times. Hence, piece-a-cake. And of course it *would* have been a piece-a-cake, if pieces of cake were huge surreal exhausting (but fun) things. Maybe it's like a Friendly Giant's piece of cake.

So if you suspect that you're a group two type of person, and if you ever find yourself putting a foot on step number one of Jacob's Ladder in Jamestown, and if you're made of The Right Stuff (78% bold idiot, 22% carbonated caffeine beverage), and if you actually make it all the way to the top, *please heed the following warning:* NEVER, under any circumstances, EVER, turn around and SKIP GAILY AND SPEEDILY DOWN thinking (stupidly) how it's so much easier to go *down* than *up*. If you ignore this warning and do this crazy thing, the next day you'll wake to find that all the muscle, blood, bone and flesh cells of your legs have been replaced – at the cellular level – with wood. Not ordinary wood. Special wood that fills you with intense pain if you (boldly or idiotically) attempt to move it.

Perhaps by now you're beginning to get some idea of the scale of Jacob's Ladder, but you may be wondering why on earth anybody ever built it. It may surprise you to learn that it was not originally constructed as a device for torturing over-confident show-off tourists. Built way back in 1829, it was originally a "vertical railway." It had a staircase in the middle and railroad tracks on each side. Little carts travelled on the tracks. At the top, three bored donkeys walked round and round in a circle, turning a capstan, which wound up ropes that hauled the little carts up.

The purpose of the vertical railway was to haul Jamestown's horse and donkey manure to the top where it was used to fertilize the fields high above the town. But manure-cart space could also be rented by citizens wanting to haul things other than manure up to their country homes. Things like groceries and household items. All this was before the discovery of germs and the invention of the word "i-i-ick!"

But eventually someone figured out that watching cart-loads of poo rise above town is not as aesthetically pleasing as watching smug, health-flaunting tourists crumple into a near-death-experience on stair #426. So they took out the railroad tracks, leaving just the stairs. This turned out to be a smart move, since today there are no horses on the island, and no donkeys in Jamestown, and as a result, no manure to be hauled, whereas there *is* the odd tourist in need of a lesson in humility.

And The Government Plan today on St. Helena is the same as The Government Plan today everywhere: to stimulate the "somewhat sluggish" (read comatose) economy by Developing The Tourist Trade. Wisely, they see Jacob's Ladder as a tourist attraction, but in my opinion, they are not maximizing The Ladder's full potential. What they *are* using it for is for "The Ladder Challenge." What they *aren't* using it for is for "The World Famous High Noon Soup Show."

Let's look first at "The Ladder Challenge," since it actually exists.

It is a timed race up The Ladder. The island's sports association advertises this once-every-two-years event abroad, and it attracts a handful of athletes from South Africa and sometimes the odd Brit. They all dream of beating the record set in 2001 by Jean-Paul Van Belle, a South African. He went up in 5 minutes 42.06 seconds. The fastest Saint time is currently held by Clayton Thomas at 6 minutes11.46 seconds. I myself can toss off a trip up in about half an hour.

I have watched The Ladder Challenge and enjoyed it immensely. It's a really great spectator sport if you know how to watch it and what to watch for. If you're ever lucky enough to see The Ladder Challenge, make sure you watch it from the top. Because at the top, as you watch each contestant crawl up the 699th step, you can see the exact same look expressed on the different faces; the look that says "Please kill me." Very entertaining, I assure you.

So I'm all for The Ladder Challenge, but I'm

convinced that Jacob's Ladder can do much more to stimulate a tourist trade on St. Helena. Jacob's Ladder could also become home to The World Famous High Noon Soup Show.

The World Famous High Noon Soup Show or "WFHN double S" is not yet world famous, only because up until now it has existed only in my mind. Hopefully, some keen-to-get-knighted civil servant in the St. Helena Government will read this, see the enormous value of the WFHN double S, and make it a reality. Then you can join the stampede to St. Helena and see the show for yourself.

People of all ages, creeds, colours, and levels of mental health will be dazzled by the WFHN double S. But those with a knowledge of its historical origin will have an even richer experience.

So here are the true historical facts that are the inspiration for the WFHN double S. Apparently, long ago, when The British Empire was in its heyday, there existed a small garrison of "redcoats" on St. Helena. Some of these soldiers guarded a fort in Jamestown, while others kept a lookout to sea from the cliffs high above at the top of Jacob's Ladder. Military planning then being much the same as it is today, the cook and the kitchen were situated at the *top* of the Ladder, and hungry soldiers were situated *below*, at the *bottom* of The Ladder. So each day at noon, a low-ranking member of The Catering Corp would be assigned to soup delivery detail. This person would probably be someone disliked because of his disgusting personal habits.

Now just imagine for a moment that this was you (and here I'm not suggesting that you have disgusting personal habits. I'm only trying to put you into the action and thereby make history come alive for you). Anyway, if it was *your* turn to deliver the soup, the cook would wrap a towel around your midriff and order you to lie face up across the two handrails at the top of The Ladder, with your back resting on one handrail and your legs resting across the other handrail. I say "resting," but because *you would be lying across the handrails at the very top of a very, VERY steep fifty-eight-storey staircase,* I don't think you'd really be doing much "resting." As soon as you were in position, the cook would set a hot tureen (large covered bowl) of hot soup on top of your towel-wrapped stomach. Then he'd tie the tureen on to you with another towel. It would be time to deliver the hot soup to the waiting soldiers, who would look like tiny red ants fifty-eight-stories below.

(Don't look down.)

Try taking heart from the thought that if you wipe out, the hot soup, being a liquid, will extinguish *most* of the friction-generated flames that will surely engulf the pin-wheeling fragments of your disintegrating body. Another cheerful thought to think at this moment might be that, one way or another, it'll all be over soon. The cook launches you with just the gentlest, tiniest push

... and you're on your way.

                    W
                     H
                      E
                       E
                        E
                         E
                          E
                           E
                            E
                             E
                              E
                               E
                                E
                                 E
                                  E
                                   E
                                    E
                                     E
                                      E
                                       E
                                        E
                                         E
                                          E
                                           E

This is the kind of activity that the word *exhilarating* was invented for.

And so, in the interest of developing tourism on St. Helena, my idea is to re-create this exciting historical event every day at noon. I see it like this: Each morning at 11:45, six Authentically Dressed British Garrison Redcoat Impersonators assemble at the base of Jacob's Ladder. Four have military snare drums, one has a pair of big-noise hand-held cymbals, and one is empty-handed and, of course, wearing an officer's uniform. The drummers stand at attention, facing each other in rows of two, shoulder to shoulder, separated by the bottom step of The Ladder. The cymbalist stands stock-still between the two rows of drummers, facing the Ladder, cymbals raised and poised in front of him. The Officer stands behind the cymbalist, with his open palm raised and poised above the cymbalist's head.

Tourists who have been milling around Parade Square gravitate toward the brightly dressed period-costumed "Living History Interpreters" (Redcoat Impersonators) standing by The Ladder. The tourists start up their videocams. An expectant hush falls over the square as high overhead we hear the faint ranting of military order-shrieking gibberish. Two men, dressed in white cook's uniforms appear as tiny white dots at the top of The Ladder. The tourists all hit the zoom lens on the video cams, and they watch as one man lies across the handrails. The second man ties a big bowl onto the first man's stomach. A nervous murmur of controlled panic washes through the crowd. The bright hot sunshine is intense. Pigeons, fairy terns and mynah birds call lazily to each other about birdly things. Their complete indifference to the impending event serves only to heighten the drama. For one long moment time stands perfectly still.

Then the drummers start the long, ominous, "here-comes-the-high-divin'-act" drum roll. The white dot spanning the handrails at the top of The Ladder suddenly drops toward town. At this precise second, The Officer signals the cymbalist by slapping the top of his head, and the cymbalist smashes the cymbals together once, with force. The Soup Man plummets down the handrails as the crowd collectively gasps involuntarily. Seconds later, The Soup Man arrives at the bottom of The Ladder, coming to a sudden perfect stop, pressing his smoking shoe against the handrail as a brake, in the time-honoured manner. At the precise moment that The Soup Man stops, The Officer again slaps the cymbalist's head, the cymbalist re-smashes the cymbals and the drum-roll abruptly ends. The crowd claps and cheers with exuberant tension-releasing relief. The soup is untied from The Soup Man's stomach and is served out among the happy-to-have-seen-it-with-their-own-videocam tourists, who just can't wait to get home and show the footage to their neighbours. And thus (ta-da-da!) every day Jacob's Ladder is transformed into a must-see, world-famous, photogenic, costumed spectacle and event.

Now I know what you're thinking. You're thinking, yeah great, but who's going to be stupid enough to be The Soup Man? Well, casting the role of The Soup Man may not be as hard as you might think. Many generations of kids on St. Helena have routinely slid down The Ladder's handrails (with surprisingly few tragedies). So to the Saints, it's a "piece-a-cake." And if I can't find anyone to do it, maybe I'll take the job myself. "Fifty-Eight-Storey Bannister-Sliding Soup Delivery Man" would look good on my résumé. And I've already got the pre-requisite disgusting personal habits.

But in the unlikely event that The World Famous High Noon Soup Show should fail to draw mass tourism to St. Helena, there's yet *another* way for Jacob's Ladder to take the island from obscurity to household-word status. The concept relies on The Big World's never-ending appetite for fads.

The Big World's never-ending appetite for fads is *so* voracious that fad-creators, even working right through Groundhog Day and Sewage Awareness Week, can't always keep up with the demand. This periodically results in uncomfortable lulls. At such times, desperation drives The Big World to recycle *old* fads.

My plan is to have the Saints team up with a certain toy manufacturer, then to wait patiently and quietly for a fad-lull, and then to cunningly re-introduce... *The Slinky*.

For those of you who missed the planet-wide Slinky craze of 1961, I shall explain. The Slinky was a spiral metal coil that could do two (yes! two!) things. It could make a chinka-chinka sound when you balanced it from palm to palm. This was, as I recall, marginally more entertaining than petting a pet rock. But the Slinky could also do something that really was kind of fascinating. *It could walk down stairs.* Perhaps by now you can see where all this is headed.

Jacob's Ladder, Jamestown, Island Of St. Helena, South Atlantic Ocean: PLANETARY CAPITAL OF THE NEW(ish) SLINKY CRAZE.

And here's how to kick-start MASSIVE MONSTER SLINKY MANIA: Have the following ad grace The Free World's television screens a minimum of sixty pillion times per hour, night and day, everyday, until all children everywhere solemnly understand that unless they get a Slinky RIGHT NOW, their entire lives will be RUINED.

Now the ad:

In the first scene, it is early morning. We hear a rooster crowing. We see the top ten steps of Jacob's Ladder, but no more. On each step in the frame a St. Helenian kid is sitting to one side of the staircase, looking at the camera. A sub-title appears and stays on the lower screen throughout the ad. It reads: *Jacob's Ladder, Island of St. Helena, South Atlantic Ocean.* The rythmic "chinka-chinka" sound of slinkys being balanced from palm to palm starts.

CLOSE-UP: a child's hand tips the slinky over the edge of the top step.

One kid starts singing The Traditional TV Ad Slinky Song:

"Who walks the stairs without a care
and leaps so high in the air?"

The camera starts panning down The Ladder, following the progress of the Slinky. Each singing kid's face lights up when he or she sees the slinky walk past his or her step. New kids come into the frame from the bottom; the ones we've already seen disappear out of the top of the frame. The appearance of each new kid adds another voice to the song.

"So pretty and bright, everyone's right,
Everyone wants a Slinky."

The camera continues panning down The Ladder; The Slinky continues to walk down the stairs past each delighted singing kid. Another line of text is now added to the sub-title: 699 *stairs*. The camera-panning continues. The Slinky-walking continues. The kids choir is a huge roar now:

"A Slinky! A Slinky!
The Wonderful Wonderful Toy!
A Slinky! A Slinky!
The fave-rit of girls and boys!"

By means of a distant camera shot, we see Jacob's Ladder in its entirety. It is now evening; the sun is setting over the South Atlantic; stars are appearing in the darkening sky. We return to the close-up panning down The Ladder, following the Slinky's progress past now-tired, still-singing kids:

"Everyone wants a Slinky,
Why don't you get a Slinky?
You oughta get a Sli-i-i-inky."

The kid on the bottom step is asleep. He is woken up, bleary-eyed and surprised, by the Slinky's arrival, just as the song and the chinka-chinka accompaniment ends. Picture fades, sub-title remains: *Jacob's Ladder, Island Of St. Helena, South Atlantic Ocean, 699 steps.*

-- End of ad --

Be smart. Sell all your worldly possessions and run out and buy Slinky shares NOW.

And if by some strange fluke, the predicted St. Helena Slinky Mass-Mania fails to materialize, come to St. Helena anyway. You gotta see Jacob's Ladder.

Step right up.

Chapter Eight

The Curse of the Emperor
(Exile Without a Smile)

Something that you won't find mentioned in any glossy tourist brochure is that Napoleon put a curse on St. Helena.

I didn't find out about it until we moved here.

Every now and then something on the island would malfunction – like, say, one of the wind turbine power generators – and someone would look ominous and say "Napoleon's curse."

But I took no real notice because I'd stopped believing in curses in 1976, when my curse on disco music failed so spectacularly. It was not until I began writing this book that I discovered that not all curses are created equal.

The method that I developed for writing this book was this: every day, I'd sit at the kitchen table, and I'd either write stuff down or I'd stare out the kitchen window, trying to think of stuff to write down. Eventually I noticed that when I looked out the window, my gaze would usually be magnetically drawn to a particular house across the valley. The house that drew my attention is a bit larger than the cottages that dot the landscape, and it's surrounded by tall evergreen trees.

I also noticed that before long my thoughts would

drift away from what I was writing about and onto the prisoner who lived – and died – in that house.

During his lifetime he had risen from obscurity to become the most powerful and feared person on this planet. He was obsessed with ruling the entire earth and was able to charm millions of people into rallying around him, ready to kill or be killed in the struggle to achieve his insane goal.

At the time, the British Government considered his conduct to be "fatal to the happiness of the world," and, after much bloodshed, the dangerous little man was forced to live in exile, here on the remote island of St. Helena. And it was here – cut off from his adoring fans, his obedient armies and his lavish palaces – that he pouted.

He made a point of hating St. Helena.

He was permitted to travel around on the island, but instead he chose, for the most part, to remain inside that house. Perhaps he feared that seeing the many splendid sights of this lovely island might interfere with his hatred of it. To him, St. Helena was a prison. And he did all he could to create prison-like conditions for himself. He shut himself away in the darkness of that house, peeking out at a very limited world through peepholes that he cut in the window shutters.

Portrait of Napoleon on St. Helena
by the author

For six long years he nursed his hatred and bitterness, and according to local folklore, he lashed out with the only weapon available to him – an evil curse. It is said that Napoleon Bonaparte cursed the Island of St. Helena *for all time,* and that *he doomed all endeavors on the island to failure.*

The sight of that house and thoughts about the curse continued to distract me from my writing. So one day I gave up and went instead to the Public Library in Jamestown to find out what I could about the curse.

I was surprised that the historic record does indeed show a long and impressive list of failures on St. Helena since The Emperor died in that house in 1821. On this tiny island there has been a failed silkworm breeding industry, a failed whale fishery, failed flax production, a failed lace-making industry, a failed mackerel cannery, a failed cinchona plantation, a failed rope and twine factory, a failed lily bulb export industry, a failed dairy and a failed brewery... to name just a few.

But it's not just the number of failures that impresses. It's the impressive *strangeness* of the failures as well. Take for example, the failure of the mackerel cannery. I quote Philip Gosse, author of the island's authoritative history textbook, *St. Helena 1502 – 1938*.

"When the colony was in the deepest of social and financial depression came a bolt from the blue, in the unexpected form of the philanthropic Mr. A. Mosely, C.M.G.

Mr. Mosely was rich. He loved St. Helena and he loved the St. Helenians and was determined to help them. He also was a man of ideas. He saw that the blue sea surrounding the island teemed with fish, particularly mackerel, and he decided to set up a factory where the freshly caught fish might be canned for export to other lands, and so bring work and wages to St. Helena. Mr. Mosely spared no expense, he brought out experts to advise him: fish experts, canning experts, every sort of expert who might be of assistance.

On the 26th February, 1909, the canning factory was duly

opened at Jamestown. Everyone was ready to play his part in making it a success.

But no one, not even the expensive experts, had reckoned on the unaccountable behavior of the mackerel. Everything had been thought out and provided for. Mr. Mosely had bought new fishing boats, and fishing gear. Fishermen had been engaged, the factory built, the new machinery was in order, the empty tins in thousands were there in which the mackerel were to be hermetically sealed.

And there were no mackerel! *Never before had there been no mackerel. The experts were unable to offer any explanation of this sudden lack of mackerel;* (my italics)

…For ten months the factory and the canners waited in vain for any mackerel to can, then the factory was shut down, and yet another scheme to help St. Helena had failed."

Stories like this impressed me, but they didn't convert me into an Emperor's Curse Believer. They did, however, nudge me along the path to it. The research left me thinking that if curses *do* exist: 1) Napoleon had some pretty hefty licks and 2) too bad disco music hadn't been invented on St. Helena.

I returned to my daily habit of sitting at the kitchen table, trying to write this book. But now it seemed… it *felt* … different. I thought I could sometimes sense a sort of *presence* in the kitchen. A cold, disapproving, menacing presence. And I noticed something else. My book was getting worse.

Day in, day out, I sat and wrote badly. I turned my

back to the window. But it didn't help at all. Finally one evening, bummed and exhausted, I had to face the fact.

The book was cursed.

The mynah birds that had been squawking on the kitchen roof flew home to their nests in the big cypress tree as the sun set on the little island in the middle of the great big sea. I sat in the kitchen in darkness. And it was here – cut off from family and friends, and flush toilets, and fridges that light up inside when the door is opened – that I pouted.

For a while.

Then my Irish-blooded, dander-elevating-genes began to activate.

"Gee, what a prick this Napoleon is," I thought. "I haven't done one thing to the guy and he goes and curses my one and only book." This cursing of *everything* in a place, *forever*, began to strike me as kind of… harsh. And unfair. A little excessive. This guy's guilty of overkill, I decided.

His curse was ruining my hopes of shedding my career as a Professional Ne'er-Do-Well and becoming an author or a poet or an artist or something. *And* he was wrecking my Unpatriotic Canadian Dream of escape to a tropical island. Not the kind of thing I take lying down.

Naturally, before too long my thinking was: "So ya wanna play *hard*-ball eh? Well alright Monsieur Le Buddy Boy – TWO CAN PLAY!"

I'd never had to whup a dead guy before... but as Joni Mitchell said, life is for learning.

It was a David-and-Goliath thing and I knew it. Unknown ne'er-do-well versus world-famous ruthless brilliant military strategist (deceased). This would take some thinking.

I reviewed my research into the curse and realized that in all these years, among all the people who'd seen their efforts fail and their dreams dashed, there is no record of anyone – ever – going after the little jerk who caused it all. No one had ever gone on the *offensive*. Therefore, I reasoned, if I didn't just give up and surrender – if I fought back – *Napoleon wouldn't be expecting it!* And although *my* military strategy was learned in group snowball fights at age eleven, I recalled that surprise attack was always a very effective maneuver.

But I still had the shadowy problem of how exactly to attack a powerful curse-wielding dead guy. When no swift answer came to mind, I decided to head back to the Jamestown Library to make an in-depth study of Napoleon's St. Helena days. I had no idea what I was looking for.

And I found it.

I uncovered something *so* explosive that I knew it would blow the lid off the whole curse thing – not only off this book, but off the whole island – forever! I knew that if I revealed to the world what I'd found, the giant shadow cast by the feared and mighty warrior, and his doom-laden stranglehold curse, would be utterly deflated evermore.

But I hesitated.

Trashing great figures of history isn't my usual line of work.

I decided to give Napoleon one last chance before launching my surprise attack. I sat in the kitchen and wrote. It still stank. Without a doubt the guy was still cursing a perfectly good book that had never meant him any harm. He left me no choice.

So here it is: my research revealed that Napoleon Bonaparte had a passion for something besides swords and rifles and cannons and gunpowder, and fire and drums and flags and uniforms and battlefields, and battles and blood and gore and mass-murder and conquest and death.

It seems he also had… a much softer side. An amorous appreciation of the warm sensuous supple compound curve. The tender mound of flesh. He had, in fact… a breast fetish.

Oh big deal, you say. Oh so what, you say. What red-blooded gun-totin' soldier-guy anywhere in history *didn't* have a normal, manly, healthy interest in the upper female form? you say.

Yes but… here's the thing: Napoleon was interested in… got excited by… how to put this?

HE HAD THE HOTS FOR HIS *OWN* HOOTERS.

Now don't get me wrong. I'm not saying there's anything wrong with that. What goes on between a man and his own hooters is strictly his own business, if you ask me. To paraphrase someone from Victorian times, "I don't care what people do, as long as they don't do it in the street and frighten the horses."

But that's a big part of the problem right there. He *did* do it in the street and he *did* frighten the horses. There are scads of oil paintings of Napoleon on horseback, *hand in shirt*. Next time you're looking at one, *notice how the horse is always rearing up, with a look of wild fear in its eye*. Obviously it's terrified that other horses will see and point and say "Hey look at *that*! Lightning's got a FLAB-FONDLER on his back!"

Stable life can so quickly become a nightmare of ridicule and bullying.

I suppose that if he'd have left it at horse-frightening I'd have been tempted to just let it go. After all, what's done is done. But this ongoing nasty cursing-everything-forever stuff, this spoiling everything for everybody on St. Helena for almost two hundred years... *that's* why all this has to come out. Someone has to show the world that this guy's not as tough as he's made out to be.

And of course I can't help wondering, why me? I know I'm not the first person to question what Napoleon was doing with his hand inside his shirt all the time. Everyone who's ever looked at a picture of him "doing it" has wondered "What's that guy doing with his hand inside his shirt?" But why was there no answer to this riddle until *I* looked into it?

I don't think it serves any purpose to accuse our historians of a cover-up conspiracy. Let's just say they've been very, *very* careful to avoid placing any emphasis on the matter. But the information has been there all along.

I admit, you can't just get a book about Napoleon and turn to the index and look up "hooters." Or "melons – public fondling of." The information has been carefully entombed inside an avalanche of Napoleoniana.

But patient sifting of a vast mass of literature has revealed the irrefutable truth.

My first indication that something very odd was being deliberately downplayed, was the casual mention, in a biography of Napoleon, of an incident gleaned from the diaries of Marchand and St. Denis, two of Napoleon's loyal servants on St. Helena. I quote:

"Marchand and St. Denis rub Napoleon down with lavender water and he gazes in the mirror at his white rounded arms, his softly swelling breasts and hairless chest and says, 'Look, would I not make a beautiful woman with breasts like these?'" (The Emperor's Last Island, Julia Blackburn, p. 115).

Now, maybe you're thinking this was just some bent comment that any regular Joe might make after being in jail and deprived of women long enough. But Napoleon *wasn't* deprived of women during his incarceration on St. Helena. He *chose* to have no relations with the opposite sex while in "jail." Quote:

"Bah! Women! When you don't think about them, you don't need them." (St. Helena, Octave Aubry, p.218).

But what Napoleon *was* thinking about strikes me as... how you say?...strawnje.

Look what biographers have glossed over from the journal of Francesco Antommarchi, Napoleon's doctor on St. Helena:

"To the doctor... he also drew attention to the feminine appearance of his body with pride rather than embarrassment: 'As you can see, Doctor, beautiful arms, rounded breasts, soft white skin, not a hair... More than one beautiful lady would glory in a chest like mine.'" (Napoleon His Wives and Women, Christopher Hibbert, p.277).

Wha?

I tried being broad-minded about this. "Okay," I said to myself, "what have we *really* got here? Just a guy, expressing an appreciation for a nice set of hooters – that just happen to be his own."

...But the word "strawnje" kept haunting me.

I wondered if the stuff in these journals was actually true, or if it could just be the work of disgruntled underlings trying to defame The Emperor. But even Las Cases joins in the chorus. Las Cases was a man completely devoted to Napoleon. He selflessly followed the Emperor into exile on St. Helena. He was Napoleon's own personal historian and took down dictation daily as Napoleon recited his memoirs.

He dutifully wrote down for posterity almost everything he heard The Emperor say while on St. Helena. Las Cases worshipped the great warrior. And yet he wrote this:

"The Emperor displayed a kind of plumpness that was not typical of our sex. He occasionally remarked upon this quite cheerfully himself." (Hibbert, p.277).

Okay. I think the evidence is pretty overwhelming: melon-jolly, hand-in-shirt flab-fondler. And perhaps with this new perspective, a new generation of historians – a more forthright, objective and open generation of historians – will re-examine previously skipped-over dubious statements in the record, like this one:

"The Emperor tweaked Betsy's ear, the way he used to do with his grenadiers." (Aubry, p13).

Grenadier-tweaker, eh? *hmmm…*

So there it is. The all-powerful mighty boogey-man who could rule from beyond the grave is no more. In his place we have just another little man, with his own little peculiarities, no better and no worse than any of us.

Curse closed.

*　　　*　　　*

Needless to say, my victory over this previously

invincible evil will be hugely beneficial to the Island of St. Helena.

But it's also done a lot for me. This book is no longer cursed. (I'm sure you'll see a vast improvement in the writing in the pages to come.) And there's a tremendous personal satisfaction in having single-handedly delivered a struggling nation out from the dark torment of tyranny and into the glorious light of a far, far better tomorrow.

In recognition of this historic achievement I'm hoping to become known as Rex "Gandhi-Of-The-South-Atlantic." I asked Mrs. Gandhi-Of-The-South-Atlantic how she liked it. By way of an answer she gave me a long, solemn stare.

She must be one of those people who find hyphenated names pretentious.

Chapter Nine

Show Me a Falling Anvil and a Good Place to Stand

I'm not a practicing professional mind-reader, but I often have "hunches" that are later proved correct.

And I'm pretty sure that right now you're thinking: "Did your quest for a means of transportation on St. Helena lead you to any Deep Fried Mars Bars?"

And *now* you're thinking: "Huh?" (one outta two – not bad).

Anyway, the answer is yes.

We didn't travel to the small English town of Falmouth to buy Deep Fried Mars Bars. We went there to buy recumbent trikes. The discovery of Deep Fried Mars Bars there was just one of those little accidents, like Columbus spotting America while trying to get to China.

I've re-read what I've just written here so far, and I realize that it contains some technical terminology that not everyone may be familiar with, so I now offer the following definitions:

recumbent trike: a 3-wheeled human-powered vehicle in which the rider pedals, steers and brakes from a reclined or "recumbent" position.

Deep Fried Mars Bar: a Mars Bar that's been deep-fried.

hunches: a word in the English language that rhymes with "lunches."

At this point, we've reached a tricky spot in the telling of this tale, for there are sure to be some people who are interested in recumbent trikes and want me to go into more detail about them right away, while other people care nothing about recumbent trikes but are dying to find out everything I know about The Deep Fried Mars Bar. And there's bound to be a third, much smaller clot of readers who don't care at all about either recumbent trikes or Deep Fried Mars Bars. They'll be busy obsessing on why I didn't define hunches as "a word in the English language that rhymes with lunches and munches and crunches and bunches and brunches... *and* punches... *and* scrunches."

I think I can satisfy this last group quite quickly, so I'll do that first. I dunno why I didn't define it like that. Just lazy I guess.

Now I'll report about The Deep Fried Mars Bar, since I think most people have at least a passing interest in it; then I'll tell about our recumbent trikes. This way, people who are really into The Deep Fried Mars Bar can quit reading after I finish that topic and go off to deep-fry one, while the recumbent trike enthusiasts read on.

*   *   *

There are many fish-and-chip shops in tiny, touristy Falmouth, but when we were there in 2001, there was only one shop selling The Deep Fried Mars Bar. I think it was called "From The Smack Of The Fisherman" or "The

Fisherman's Smack" or "Fish-n-Chips-n-Heroin" or something.

I remember that it was on a short side street, down the hill from the square where the buses come and go… near *Falmouth's* Jacob's Ladder. (And here I digress to mention that, compared to St. Helena's massive, towering, Slinky-punishing 699 steps, Falmouth's Jacob's Ladder taint nuthin' but a wussy-pussy kiddies' ladderette.)

Anyway, back to "The Smack-n-Crack-n-Bennies-n-Fish" or whatever it was called. The shop was family-owned-and-run by very nice people. The first time Cynthia and I went in, it was a dark and stormy night. The tourist season was long since over, and the take-away shop had no other customers in it. The family's teenage daughter was holding down the fort. She was a Marxist Leninist Commie Pinko, but I didn't know it then, and besides, she was lovely with it.

Cynthia and I both asked for cod in batter and chips, and the young woman went about the business of deep-frying our order. With nothing much else to do in the small fluorescently-lit shop, I started reading the surprisingly long wall-mounted menu, item by item.

That's when I saw it: Deep Fried Mars Bar.

Immediately I wondered what it could be. I pondered and pondered. Finally I had to ask the girl: "What's a 'Deep Fried Mars Bar'?"

She smiled and replied, "It's a Mars Bar that's been deep fried." (It was this exchange that authorized me to state the definitive definition of The Deep Fried Mars Bar a couple of pages ago.)

So I ordered one. Cynthia and I walked to the pier and sat on a bench to eat. It was a chilly night but the rain had let up and was now just a light drizzle. We were both cold and hungry and the hot fish and chips really hit the spot. They were very filling though and when I'd finished I was stuffed. But I still had a grease-soaked paper bag sitting beside me on the bench. A grease-soaked paper bag with a Deep Fried Mars Bar in it.

I didn't really want it.

The meal we'd just eaten had been good, but in fifteen minutes I'd consumed more grease than I would normally eat in several outhouse holes. However, I don't like to waste food or money, so I made myself take a bite.

The thing was unimaginably superb.

I enthusiastically urged Cynthia to try it. She refused. She was full. C'mon, ya gotta. No thanks. I cajoled. No go. I entreated. Unh-uh. I begged. She groaned. So I pulled out my never-fail most persuasive argument: *aw, come ON*. Reluctantly, she took a bite.

When we returned to the shop to buy more I eagerly asked the girl about the provenance of the delicacy. I was prepared for her to be very guarded about it – a well-kept secret family recipe handed down from generation to generation sort of thing. But she was entirely open.

"My brother had one once somewhere up in

Scotland, so we decided to try it here in the shop," she said.

"Do lots of people order them?"

She reckoned a moment before answering.

"Yeah. They sell pretty well."

Sensing that I was rabidly interested, *she then just up and volunteered the recipe.* And although I'd just arrived from Canada where we don't have the word "gobsmacked," *I was gobsmacked!*

Obviously she cared nothing for the capitalist edge that came from being the only shop with The Deep Fried Mars Bar. She evidently adhered to the commie pinko philosophy that The Deep Fried Mars Bar is the food of The People and that we all have a collective inalienable *right* to the recipe, because it belongs to all good factory workers everywhere. So comrades, in that same spirit, I share it with you now: First, remove the Mars Bar from its wrapper. Then freeze it. (The Mars Bar, not the wrapper.) Then dip the frozen Mars Bar in typical English fish-and-chips type batter, and then deep-fry it.

The public-spirited Trotskyist food-girl worker-person explained that the freezing allows the batter on the outside to fry to crispness just as the Mars Bar on the inside reaches gooey meltedness.

*   *   *

Okay. Everybody else has gone to the store to buy Mars Bars. It's just us recumbent cyclists left now.

There was a time when I didn't even know what a

recumbent trike was. Cynthia and I were living in Canada then, just outside of Winnipeg. We'd been to St. Helena for six months, loved it, and had returned to Canada to earn money, sell up and go live on The Jewel Of The South Atlantic.

We'd sold our car and were riding bicycles all year round, to save money. And some days – when it wasn't winter – I'd see an amazing little machine hurtle down the highway past our house. It was a very sci-fi-looking thing, with a clear glass bubble over the front, and inside was a man, lying down, pedaling. Very intriguing. I often tried to catch up to him on the road, but my clunky two-wheeler was no match for his sleek little futuristic machine and he was always long gone. One day though, as I was shovelling gravel to make our driveway, I saw him zoom past. From previous observations I knew that he'd be coming back the other way, toward the city, in about 45 minutes. So when the time drew near, I stood at the side of the road and waited. When he showed, I flagged him down frantically and he stopped.

"Sorry to bother you," I said, "but I see you going by all the time and I'm just dying to know what this thing is."

"Recumbent trike," he said.

The cyclist, Pete by name, patiently answered all my questions. He told me that if I wanted to, I could look up "Human Powered Vehicles" on the internet and learn more. I sheepishly explained that I am computer illiterate and had no computer. Pete kindly offered to download some info about trikes and drop it off to us on one of his rides. He even offered to let us try a turn on his trike in the yard. My legs were too long and my knees hit against the plexiglass bubble wind fairing, so I was unable to peddle the tiny vehicle. But Cynthia was able to do a little spin around the yard, which she enjoyed.

True to his word, Pete dropped off pages from various websites and that's how we came to know about Inspired Cycle Engineering, or ICE, manufacturers of recumbent trikes in Falmouth, England.

ICE is owned and run by two honest, hardworking, brilliant, perfectionist engineers – Neil and Chris. In a small factory on the edge of Falmouth, they hand-make each machine from the ground up.

Their flawless vehicles are generally regarded as the Rolls-Royce of recumbent trikes. There is a world-wide demand for ICE trikes and the order-book is always filled far into the future. Most business people in a demand-exceeding-supply situation would hire help and expand. But not Neil and Chris. They love their work and they enjoy obsessing on each and every detail of each and every trike they build. They have chosen to remain small and to hand-build their trikes one at a time. No mass-production assembly line. No bloated corporation. No perma-stress from a life of perma-meetings. Just two guys doing what they do so well – create brilliant gleaming ingenious machines.

Cynthia and I ordered our trikes while we were still

in Canada. We explained that we were taking them to St. Helena where the roads are very, very steep, and Neil and Chris recommended a special mountain gearing. All ICE trikes come with drum brakes, (like those on motorcycles) mounted in the two front wheels. They give excellent braking power, even when plummeting down a steep winding mountain road in rainy conditions. We selected the model we wanted (The Explorer) and various options (luggage rack and 5 panniers, lights, water bottle holders, etc.) and we both picked red as the colour for the frame. We paid in advance (yes, it was expensive, but it's nice to own one really good thing isn't it? ...plus you don't have to buy petrol later on) and Neil and Chris promised to have the custom-built trikes ready and waiting for us when we arrived at Falmouth en route to St. Helena.

We arrived in Falmouth late at night, jet-lagged, train-lagged and exhausted. We were carting an absurd amount of very heavy luggage, because as passengers on the RMS *St. Helena*, we would be permitted two cubic meters of luggage each, to be delivered with us to St. Helena, included in the price of the ship ticket. (This baggage allowance has since been reduced to one cubic meter per person.) We knew that shipping stuff to the island was very expensive, and that on the island, selection was very limited and prices were very high. So we had to take full advantage of the baggage allowance. Which meant that we were both loaded down like pack donkeys all the way from Winnipeg to Falmouth.

We pulled into Falmouth on the last train that dark cold January night, and started heaving huge heavy suitcases and giant cumbersome packs and leaden shoulder bags onto the platform. We managed to chuck all the stuff off the train before the automated doors closed and the train bolted off into the night. There was no train station, just a platform, and not a soul around. We couldn't possibly carry all the stuff around Falmouth while we looked for a place to sleep for the night, so I stayed with our worldly possessions while Cynthia set off to find us a hotel room or something.

I hadn't slept on the plane from Winnipeg to Montreal. Or on the long flight across the Atlantic. Or on the endless succession of trains we'd been on since landing in London. Every train seemed to have only three or four cars, and it seemed to travel only about ten or twenty miles. Then we'd have to heave our hernia-making load off, cart it all across a bunch of train tracks and up and down a few flights of stairs, and assemble it all beside another platform in yet another grotty train station, to wait an hour or two for another dinky, short-run train and repeat the whole nightmare all over again. The sheer insanity of the train system finally prompted me to do the unthinkable in Britain: I spoke to A Total Stranger… to ask why the hell the train system was so demented. After recovering from shock, The Total Stranger quickly explained that the system had been privatized and sold off in little tiny pieces to a zillion different companies who all hated each other and showed this by refusing to co-ordinate any of their routes or schedules. Then The Total Stranger scuttled off, amazed at having survived a verbal exchange with Someone He Didn't Know.

Now it was midnight. A light drizzle began to fall. The Falmouth railroad platform had no roof. I sat alone among our bags in the dark, dampening slowly. Fortunately I had reached that stage of exhaustion where nothing bothers you, because everything is surreal, and you are long past caring. Several centuries later Cynthia showed up.

"I found a Bed and Breakfast," she said.

We had so much stuff to carry, and we were so tired, that we had to move everything in relay fashion, a few bags at a time. So, in back-and-forth twenty-step stints, we headed down the street – to the very last house on the street of course. Fortunately, the very last house on the street, The Moonlight B&B, was the most welcoming, friendliest, most caring, most helpful place I've ever stayed.

After a big huge sleep and a Cornish Pasty breakfast (and here I'll not digress to justify my love affair with the delicious Cornish Pasty. I'll just point out that there are cars driving around Falmouth with bumper stickers that say "NO HAND SIGNALS – I'M EATING A PASTY.") Anyway, after breakfasting on the first of many memorable mouth-watering pasties, we phoned ICE and got directions.

Cynthia and I enjoyed our walk across the town of Falmouth. It's very scenic – hilly, with interesting architecture. When we reached the edge of town, we located ICE, at the rear of a small building in an industrial park. Neil and Chris welcomed us to their tiny factory, and presented us with our trikes – which were, inarguably, drop-dead gorgeous.

We wheeled them out into the parking lot (the trikes, not Neil and Chris, who are younger than us) and Neil and Chris explained how to get on them and off them (again, the trikes, not Neil and Chris) and how to steer and brake and change gears.

Riding a recumbent trike is exhilarating for several reasons. You sit very low to the ground, so it *feels* very fast. But the low center of gravity makes it seem safe, like a formula one racing car. And having three wheels adds to the safe feeling because you can't fall over, as on a two wheeled bike. This not-having-to-balance frees up the Balance Lobe in the rider's brain, so that it no longer has to think "Left… a bit more left… now right… quick! More right!" The Balance Lobe can instead think "WooHoo!"

After an hour or so in the parking lot, Cynthia and I had a pretty good idea of how to, and we were ready for the open road.

Almost.

On our way to the ICE factory, we'd come across

several bustling traffic-filled roundabouts, and I thought I'd better just ask if there was anything that we should know about roundabouts before heading out, because we'd never been on one before.

"Is there anything that we should know about roundabouts before heading out? We've never been on one before," I said.

Neil and Chris exchanged a look of concern and apprehension. After a brief, tense silence Chris said, "Maybe we should step into the office so I can explain something."

We filed into their cramped narrow office and perched on boxes and grubby grease-slimed folding chairs. Chris stood in front of a wall-mounted chalkboard that was covered with technical drawings and figures. These he erased. Then he drew a circle on the board and began to speak in an upbeat, professor-like tone.

"This," he said, pointing to the circle, "is an English roundabout. English road planners introduced the roundabout as a way of directing uninterrupted traffic flow without using expensive, land-consuming overpasses and underpasses and on-ramps and exit-ramps. When approaching a roundabout, look to your right. The vehicle to your right has the right of way. If there *is* no vehicle to your right you can proceed into the roundabout without stopping."

Chris had been erasing sections of the circle, to indicate incoming roads, and was now drawing curved arrows entering and exiting the circle. He was babbling something about which lane to travel in within the roundabout and drawing spirals and circles and more bent arrows inside the circle. My mind scanned the diagram on the blackboard, flashed back to high school Physics class, and immediately shut down.

When I regained consciousness a few minutes later, the diagram resembled busy, unpleasant abstract art and Chris was saying, "So in that case you just hand-signal and proceed to the outermost lane and exit. Alright?"

"Yeah, I think so," I lied. I was thinking, I hope Cynthia understood some of this.

I thought that was the end of it and that we could get out of there and start bombing around on our beautiful new trikes. I was just about to thank Chris and stand up when he suddenly looked deathly serious and started speaking again, this time in a low, warning tone.

"Being from Canada, you can't be expected to know much about this next bit, so I'll start at the beginning. We are in Cornwall," he said, "and for hundreds of years, Cornwall did not consider itself to be part of England. It's only become a part of England in relatively recent history, and the Cornish people still think of themselves as *different* from the English. The Cornish think they're seen by the English as poor country cousins." (I must say that I found all this interesting, but I wanted to hit the road on my sparkling red three-wheeler.)

"So," Chris continued, "you might say that The

Cornish developed a sort of inferiority complex somewhere along the line, and a *competition* evolved in the Cornish mind. Cornish versus English. A whatever-the-English-can-do-we-can-do-better sort of thing." (Here I suddenly remembered that Chris and Neil had mentioned that they'd both moved to Cornwall from other areas of England because they liked the beautiful Cornish countryside, the mild climate, the surfing on the ocean and the nice vibe of the Cornish people. This meant that Neil and Chris were *transplanted Englishmen*. I stored this data on a back-burning lobe and tuned Chris in again.)

"...So when English road planners introduced the roundabout, the Cornish, of course, looked on and said, "We can do better."

He turned around and erased the crazy diagram. Then he drew two circles, one above the other.

"This," he said, "is the Cornish *Double* Roundabout." He let the terror of that soak in for a second and then said, "When you come to one of these, you just do what everyone else does – close your eyes, pray, and go as fast as you can."

And armed with this wisdom, Cynthia and I spent a couple of very enjoyable weeks triking through scenic Cornwall. The landscape is remarkably similar to parts of St. Helena, and it was a perfect proving ground for future triking on the island.

There's no bicycle shop on St. Helena so Chris very

generously gave us a crash course in trike mechanics, and, loaded up further with the most-likely-to-wear-out spare parts, we headed to Cardiff to catch the RMS *St. Helena*.

*　　*　　*

A few weeks later I was standing in the tropical sun on the wing of the bridge, absently watching the bow smash through the waves of the huge empty ocean. I had been lost in a reverie and was suddenly brought back to the present by the realization that a grumpy woman passenger was staring disapprovingly at me with that "are you on drugs?" stare that I'm so familiar with. I knew I'd been grinning idiotically. I had been remembering the down-home little office at ICE, and the map of the world that Chris and Neil have on the wall there. The entire map is plastered with pins with little flags on them, each representing a spot where they've shipped a trike to a customer. It had reminded me of the black-and-white late movies I'd seen about the second world war and I liked it. It struck me as a very plucky British World War Two good-show-old-boy sort of thing. And I'd been remembering my strange sense of pride and pleasure the day that Neil stuck a little flag into a fly-speck in the South Atlantic Ocean.

No Ma'am, I'm not on drugs. I'd explain the look on my face to you, but it's kind of a long story. Ever heard of recumbent trikes? Deep Fried Mars Bars? No? Well, some other time perhaps.

*　　*　　*

Cynthia and I have been triking St. Helena for almost five years now – and loving it.

Triking St. Helena is like surfing Hawaii. You ride the big ones. What St. Helena lacks in surfable ocean waves it more than makes up for in seriously steep, winding, downhill freewheelin' Big Kahuna triking roads.

First, you pedal the long slow ascent (triking's answer to paddling a surfboard way out to where the big waves curl). And it's on the long uphill climb that the trike has it over the two-wheeled bicycle. On a bike, if you can't get enough speed up, you can't balance the machine, and it wobbles and then falls over. So on a really steep ascent, you soon have to get off and push your bike to the top. Not so the trike. No matter how steep or long the climb, we never have to get off and push. The trike doesn't have to be balanced, so we can go, in a nice un-wobbly straight line, as slow as we want. So Cynthia and I trike a ways, stop, put on the parking brake, drink water, rest in the comfortable seat, chat, then go again until we reach either the next rest stop, or the top. And when we finally do reach the top, "Surf's up!"

And just like in surfing, you can get addicted to the rush and end up building your whole life around it.

By rights, triking should have its own music, just like surfing has surf music. Trike music would have to be peppy, upbeat and fun-sounding. But instead of being about surfboards and customized cars and surfer-girls it would be all about recumbent trikes.

Brian Wilson, do you read me?

I'm not big on the idea of trike-flavoured *Beach Blanket Bingo*-type movies though. I may be alone in this, but I always thought those surf movies were just an itsy bitsy, teenie weenie bit (Frankie Avalon, forgive me!) *shallow*.

*   *   *

Cynthia on the road between Levelwood and Rock Rose

The Saints had never seen a recumbent trike before and needless to say, at first there was a bit of an atmosphere of the-circus-has-come-to-town.

I remember one day, Cynthia and I were triking the steep climb home from Jamestown. A car approaching us stopped and a woman got out, looking amused and intrigued. She opened her purse and started rummaging through it as she asked, "What's this in aid of?" We responded by looking blank. She stopped rummaging and looked up. "Aren't you-all fund raising for some cause?" she asked, confused.

"No. We're going home," we answered, confused. Confusion is natural when someone mistakes you-going-home for a zany fund raising stunt.

But soon everybody adjusted and the island's courteous drivers just honked and waved like they would if we were driving ordinary vehicles.

Cynthia and I often stopped to chat with the friendly gangs of workmen that repair the island's roads – unless it meant interrupting a thrilling downhill free-wheel. In those situations we'd just zoom past and wave. The men always joyfully yelled something at us, but for years I couldn't understand what it was they were shouting.

"Blowdee Whodah! Blowdee Whodah!" – said very fast – almost all one syllable.

One day I finally figured it out: "Blow... the... hooter!" They wanted me to honk the trike's powerfully loud air-horn. It was cultural differences that had made this so hard for me to decipher. I was raised Canadian, where a vehicle's audio warning device is called a *horn*, not a hooter. To us Canadians, a *hooter* is a lump of male chest flab.

*   *   *

Cynthia and I are lucky in that we share so many of the same interests, such as triking. For her, triking as an adult is as natural as can be, because one of her happiest memories of childhood is of riding her tricycle down the sidewalk in Winnipeg. She tells me she used to wear a sweater on her head, with the sleeves draping down onto her shoulders, and she'd hop on her tricycle and ride as fast as she could so that her long "hair" would fly in the breeze. To this day, her face glazes over in fond recollection of it.

As adults, we see eye to eye on so many things... yet we have very different recollections of childhood.

*   *   *

The children where I grew up were the same as children everywhere – bloodthirsty and sadistic.

So anytime word got out that I was attempting to learn to ride a bicycle, they'd all drop everything and come running to razz and jeer and delight in my spectacular crashes and self-inflicted wounds.

My performances were the stuff of local legend, partly because I was so entertainingly uncoordinated, and partly because I was so hilariously grim and determined. The Watch Rex Crash Show enjoyed a long run. I was summer-stock theatre, revived year after year – a local old favourite. I wanted to ride a bike *so* badly, but the trick of balancing the thing was, to me, a complete mystery.

I'm not exactly sure why, but my older brother tried hard to teach me to ride. Perhaps he felt sorry for me, or perhaps he wanted to end the social stigma of being the brother of the neighbourhood joke, or perhaps he was attracted to the problem because it seemed to call for his favourite remedy – stubborn repetition.

At the time, he was breeding budgies for profit and had invested heavily in a 45 RPM record that was "Guaranteed To Teach Budgies To Talk," according to the record jacket. Robert shrewdly reasoned that talking budgies would be worth much more than non-talking ones, so he stubbornly played and replayed the record, which obnoxiously repeated things like "Hello" and "How are you?" in bird-voice over and over and over again ad nauseum. Robert never gave up. But mercifully the record finally did. It wore out before any of his budgies had even learned to say "rip-off."

Maybe Robert thought that teaching me to ride a bike was like teaching a budgie to talk – a challenging Frankensteinian/Dr.Moreau-type experiment in pushing the known boundaries of nature. He may have reasoned that what came *naturally* to a gangly, awkward, uncoordinated kid was *crashing* a bike... but, through Stubborn Repetition, such a kid might be trained to *ride* a bike... and if the natural order of things could thus be reshaped, ergo it may *also* follow that someday his budgies would talk, and his fortune would be made.

I have never really learned what his motivation was, but the fact remains that he spent a great many hours running along beside me, holding onto the seat with one hand and the handlebars with the other, giving instruction. Unfortunately, trying to tell someone how to balance a moving bicycle is a bit like trying to tell someone how to bend notes on a harmonica. Words can convey only so much and no more.

Eventually, Robert would let go and watch as I inevitably wobbled, then slalomed, then drunkenly zig-zagged, getting more and more out of control with each frantic spin of the pedals until I finally reached the panic-filled sensational crash.

Although he is only one year older than me, Robert treated the problem with almost adult seriousness, like a professional coach, analyzing the cause of each crash and offering tips on how to prevent the next one. He disregarded my bloody skinned knees, hands, and elbows, and the lumps and bruises on my head, just as he disregarded the jubilant heckling children who ran to the scene of each crash to joyfully inspect the damage I'd done to myself and the bike. My brother would just calmly ask, "You wanna try again?" Fighting back the tears (as best I could), ignoring the stinging pain of the scrapes (as best I could), and shutting out the taunts and insults of the unwanted audience (as best I could), I'd get on and try again.

The neighbourhood kids never tired of this action-drama, and as I've said, it went on for years. There were kids half my size who could ride a two-wheeler, and as soon as a kid mastered the art of it, he or she was, by Children's Law, entitled to full jeering rights. So not only was the audience ever-expanding, it also presented the unusual phenomenon of little kids taunting a bigger kid.

Oh the shame of it all!

But I do remember very clearly, even after forty-one years, the magic day when the ordeal ended. It began in ordinariness, like any other day. Everything was the same as it always was: the back-lane location, scene of countless painful wipe-outs; the tireless jibes of the eager audience; the start, with my brother assisting; the letting go; the familiar fear of crashing and the familiar nagging worry that I was weird and abnormal. And then *I didn't crash!* I kept going. When I wobbled, I *corrected* it. I *steered*. If I wanted to go in a direction, I just steered toward it and the bike actually *went* there. After going the entire block of the back-lane unscathed, I came to a controlled stop.

I felt like I was in a wonderful dream as I got off and walked the bike in a U-turn, facing my brother and the crowd of startled dumb-struck children. I got on. I pedalled. I balanced. I steered. I rode right up to them. Right past them. Right out onto the street. All the way around Peanut Park! I realized then that this wasn't some lucky fluke. I finally, really, possessed the skill and the knowledge. I could do it.

I could ride a bike.

To me it was like suddenly being able to fly. It was not only a glorious moment, it was the doorway to glorious hours, days, weeks and years. Every day after school I went riding, usually alone. I rode far and wide, going much further than I ever did walking. I travelled, sight-seeing. I could go anywhere, and I felt so free.

I've never lost the feeling that me-riding-a-bicycle is some sort of miracle.

*   *   *

And it was my skill as a cyclist that got me my big break in the movie business when I was seventeen. Actually it was my cycling skill combined with my willingness to work all summer "wage-unfettered" (as I choose to call it) that got me my job as Movie-Star-Without-Pay.

My oldest sister, Lorna, introduced me to her friend, an aspiring young writer/producer/director, who told me he was looking to hire a movie-star, cheap. *Real* cheap. Without pay, in fact. Perhaps it was my budding career as a Professional Ne'er-Do-Well that suggested to them that I may be suitable to fill the post. The main qualification for the position was the "without-pay" part, with a special consideration given to those applicants who could also ride a bicycle. Of course I was swiftly thinking, "Hey, this job has *me* written all over it... *for I can ride a bicycle!*"

The friend's name was Kenny Finkleman. He had an offbeat sense of humour and I liked him right away, as most people do, I think. He was a wild and crazy '60s radical who liked to get up and *do* stuff.

I asked Kenny what the movie would be about. He told me good-humouredly that he wasn't sure yet, because he was still writing it. Then he became very, very serious. He had one *very* serious point to make to me. He could not stress the seriousness of this point enough. His serious point was this: If I started the movie, I *had* to finish it. He was investing his every last dime making this movie (not on actors' salaries though) and he could not afford to start over again if the Movie-Star-Without-Pay quit to hitchhike to BC to pick peaches or something. So I solemnly committed to star in a movie about... something... to be filmed full-time over the summer months in Winnipeg, for a salary negotiated to be... nothing.

A couple of weeks later we started shooting. The gist of the movie was that I was a young radical. In scene after scene I'd ride up and down dingy downtown alleyways on an old bicycle. I'd stop in front of an old brick wall, get off and remove a large paintbrush and a gallon of white paint from a handlebar basket on the bike. Then I'd paint a political slogan on the wall in bold four-foot-high letters. At the time, the Viet Nam war was on, and I was to paint stuff like "PIGS OUT OF SOUTH EAST ASIA" and "POWER COMES OUT OF THE BARREL OF A GUN" and so forth. Kenny had scouted each scene location and gotten permission from the building owners to paint on the walls. (The paint was washable.)

Shooting went pleasantly enough and uneventfully until one bright and sunny morning several weeks into the thing. We were in an alley in what is now called The Exchange District – an area so named because it had housed the grain-exchange business in Winnipeg's past, selling Manitoba's huge wheat crop for export all over the world. The architecture of the area was and still is Gangster-Era Chicago.

In recent times, the Canadian Government has done much to develop the film-making industry in Manitoba: creating a government bureau to promote the province and the city as shooting locations, offering tax incentives to lure Hollywood movie-makers north, and preserving the buildings of The Exchange District. Nowadays the area frequently appears in American movies, standing in for American cities of the 1920s and 1930s.

But back in the 1960s, there was no government funding or promotion. There was only the odd rare nut making a movie on a shoestring. By the standards of the day, Kenny's movie project was big-time. He had (some) authentic Hollywood equipment and (at times) up to about a dozen people on the (volunteer, unpaid) crew.

And Kenny himself came across like what we Provincial Prairie Bumpkins imagined an Authentic Hollywood Producer/Director would be like. He had a built-in smirk that suggested that everyone but him was an amusing idiot. He was intense, crazy and persuasive. He was high-energy. He talked fast and convincingly, and actually smoked cigars. He was not your average prairie-town boy.

So we were in this alley. The crew got everything ready for the scene. It was about eleven a.m. I was briefed as to what the scene was to be. I was to ride up to such-and-such a spot, get off, look at the wall, get out the paint and the brush and paint this slogan on the wall: "BREAK EVERY LAW – INCLUDING THE LAW OF GRAVITY."

Got it, yup, no problem. I did as directed. I painted as far as "BREAK EVERY LAW" and the camera ran out of film. A discussion ensued. What to do? Go get more film and resume? Or? Kenny eventually decided he wanted to look at "the rushes" (film shot that morning and quick-developed) over at the CBC before continuing. So he took off (eh?) saying he'd be back "soon." In twos and threes the crew sloped off, loading whatever items they were responsible for into cars and vans and headed off to grab a quick bite. I was left in a deserted alley that only a few minutes before had been a bustling movie set.

Just me – leaning against a wall, enjoying the sun, with a six-inch paintbrush in my hand, dripping white paint. Me, and an old bike leaning against the wall, with a gallon of white paint sitting in the carrier, and the slogan in fresh gleaming-white four-foot-high letters on the grey brick wall.

That's what the cops saw as they cruised into the alley. They pulled up. They got out. They both looked at me, then at the wall – BREAK EVERY LAW – then at me again. Completely seriously, one of the cops asked me, "Did you do this?" I laughed. Actually I guffawed. I didn't mean to, it just came out. The question struck me as hilariously stupid. A more obvious "crime scene" probably never presented itself to police in the history of crime.

I suddenly realized that they weren't sharing my mirth. In fact, they looked disgusted and agitated.

"Yeah, of *course* I did! But see, we're making a *movie* here, so it's okay."

Both cops looked at me for what seemed like a very long time, their disgust and agitation increasing visibly. Finally one said, "Who's '*we*'?"

"Oh! The crew and everybody... the director... and the camera-man..." My voice trailed off. The cops oozed irritation as they looked up and down the empty alley. A newspaper blew along like a lonesome tumbleweed.

"Uh... we ran out of film... and then people went off... to get lunch... and... uh..."

The cops stared, very hard-faced. I made one last attempt at preventing things from getting full-on ugly.

"The painting on the wall is really okay. It's water paint – washable! The director has permission from the owner of the building. It's okay! Kenny Finkleman – that's the director – he'll be back soon."

"Who?" the cop barked.

"Kenny Finkleman."

"Never hearda no 'Kenny Finkleman'." The cop sneered at my pathetic, hallucinatory, fictional-fairy-tale-alibi of a lie. The other cop took the paintbrush from my hand and opened the back door of the cruiser.

"Get in."

"Uh... what about the bike and the brush and the paint?"

"You don't need 'em."

"Oh yeah, they'll need them for the rest of the movie. You need to keep all the same stuff for each shot!"

"GET IN!"

I got in.

The cop violently slammed the door shut and we set off for the feared and dreaded Public Safety Building a few blocks away. This was a newly-built high-rise jail, and in those Establishment-versus-Long-Hairs days, there were reports coming back to the street of beatings in the elevators between floors and such-like unsavoury events.

The cops in the front seat were sour, tough, hard-boiled pork. Righteous upholders of the thin blue line between law and order and the ever-increasing degenerate-hippie-bum-freak anarchy. And they seemed viciously pleased to have apprehended a lying nut-case hippie who had defaced a building with a huge sign urging the good citizens of their fine metropolis to "BREAK EVERY LAW."

I watched nervously as we neared the jail of ill-repute. I began to fear that I wasn't fearless.

What happened next shows that Kenny has watched plenty of TV cop shows. His car roared up alongside the police cruiser, then past it, then screeched to a halt sideways across the street, directly in front of the cruiser.

The cop driving had no choice but to slam the brakes on hard, and, tires screaming, the cop-car lurched to a dead stop. But even before it had stopped Kenny was out of his car and bounding to the driver's side of the cruiser, cigar in mouth. He stuck his head right inside the car, and, belching smoke, demanded LOUDLY, "What *is* this? That's my *STAR!* We're *SHOOTING! What the hell are you doing?*" His face and tone implied "you amusing buffoons!"

Gut instinct told the cops that this guy was for real. A *real* movie director! And therefore, the delinquent hippie-bum in the back seat must be… *a movie star?*

They sensed that all this was above board, but they were in a deep state of high-speed gear-change whiplash-shock. They stammered confused apologies to both of us. (That put me in shock.) Kenny magnanimously accepted the apologies (Hey guys, we all make mistakes) and buddy-buddied and joked with them for a minute or two. He invited them to come watch the shoot and we left, leaving the cops to wrap their heads around what this crazy world was coming to. And leaving me marvelling at the weird respect you get for this Movie-Star-Without-Pay antic.

Shooting carried on without noteable event until a few weeks later.

The location was outside the unfinished Winnipeg Art Gallery, across the street from the Hudson's Bay Company store. The Art Gallery was being built on an odd-shaped triangular lot, and the building featured an open triangular cement porch or apron in front, about four feet above sidewalk level. Construction was not yet complete and there was a deep ditch surrounding the apron, where, I suppose, pipes were going to be laid.

Kenny had gotten permission to film from the roof of the Hudson's Bay Building across the noisy traffic-clogged six-lane-wide street. My instructions were to ride in a circle round and round on the triangular apron.

Although he'd somehow gotten hold of an authentic big-time Hollywood camera, Kenny had no walkie-talkies and no way to communicate between the Art Gallery (scene of the action) and the store roof (command post), six stories above the traffic noise. (All this was in The Olden Days, before the invention of the cell phone.) Much time was spent setting up the shot, with messengers travelling back and forth between the two places. Finally shooting began.

I rode in a circle. The crew on the ground were saying "Why are they all waving their arms like that up on the roof? Kenny must want Rex to ride faster. Hey Rex! They want you to ride faster!"

I rode faster.

"Now they're waving even more. Rex! They want you to ride faster!"

So I rode faster.

This process was repeated until I was riding at high speed in a tight circle. I was thinking that if the Movie-

Star-Without-Pay profession didn't pan out, maybe I'd rent a chimpanzee suit and join a circus.

The bike was old and required a lot of oomph to get it going fast. The heavy can of paint in the handlebar basket didn't make it any easier.

"They want faster! Go faster!" I had to stand up on the pedals to achieve more speed.

Finally, near exhaustion, I made a wrong move. I looked up to see for myself what they wanted at the camera. They were, in fact, all waving frantically. I looked for only a split second, but when I looked back down at what I was doing I knew it was already too late.

As the bike bounced over a low curb and then nose-dived over the edge, the paint can lid, which had been pressed on loosely, came flying off. The paint came out and flowed right above me, over my head. I went sailing over the handlebars with my arms outstretched, in a reflex action, to break my fall. Instead I broke my wrists. Then I bounced, landing on my elbows, breaking both my arms.

I stood up. I looked at the sharp bones protruding at weird angles from the skin at my elbows. I was in shock and felt no pain at that moment. In a few minutes the crew from the roof arrived, Kenny among them.

"What happened?" he asked. "Why were you going so fast? We kept waving to get you to slow down!"

At the Victoria Hospital I was booked into a room shared with a very nice man from a small rural town, who was encased in a full body cast. I was floating very high above the pain on a Demerol injection, and was enjoying my neighbour's company.

He asked me, "What happened?"

I told him, "I fell off a bicycle."

He said, "A motorcycle?"

I said, "No. A bicycle."

Little did I know that this was the first of hundreds of times that I would have this exact same conversation, with friends, with family, with complete strangers. It was as if hundreds of different people, of all ages and from all walks of life, were auditioning for a part in a play, and they knew their lines, and I knew mine. After we got to the part where I'd say "No. A bicycle," they'd ad-lib from there, but until then, the lines were always strictly adhered to.

My roommate told me how glad he was to have someone to talk to. He had been very bored since his last roommate had been discharged a few days before. He told me how he had ended up in a full body cast and then he went on to talk about life in the little Manitoba town he was from. He was a good talker, and I was enjoying his stories, when suddenly, in burst Kenny, cigar in place (unlit).

"Hey Rex! I got them to rush the processing. We got *the whole thing!* I've seen it. It *really* looks great! Thought you'd want first look so I came right over. I gotta projector. You look like you can't move – that's okay, just stay right there, I'll set up here beside the bed and we can project onto that wall. We'll hafta close these curtains, d'you mind?" he asked my roommate.

My roommate didn't mind. He was enjoying the hub-bub and was very favourably impressed when the hospital room was suddenly transformed into a darkened movie theatre, featuring a Hollywood-quality, zoomed-in feature presentation of my accident.

We watched it once. It *was* good. Then we watched it again, in slow-motion. It was *great!* In slow-mo, I look up while riding. I look back down. I suddenly look afraid. The bike rises then tilts downward very steeply. The paint lid ejects in a beautiful outer-space-like end-over-end float. The paint erupts. My head and face are momentarily blanked out as the paint passes wavily over me. My face reappears, registering more surprise than fear now. I float over the handlebars, arms outstretched, like Superman launching into his faster-than-a-speeding-bullet flight, except that I'm flying toward the bottom of a ditch. The wrist-snapping landing looks soft, with a gentle puff of dust. The rebound is surprisingly high as I float up and then float down onto my elbows. Bones sprout from both elbows and I settle, motionless. Then I stand and observe the weird wreckage of my arms, looking almost bored.

After the slo-mo run-through Kenny opened the curtains. My roommate offered his enthusiastic congratulations on an excellent movie and a fabulous accident. He gave us a well-deserved (if I may say so myself) rave review.

Kenny asked if I needed anything, and told me not to worry about the movie, and then left. I was operated on to remove bone splinters from my arm muscles, and had my arms embedded in two armpit-to-fingertip plaster casts for twelve weeks, during which time I could not feed or wash myself or scratch the unrelenting itching inside the casts.

I was released from the hospital and that autumn, as soon as one cast was removed, I finished the movie.

Kenny didn't pressure me to. The need to finish it came from me. I had been programmed and conditioned by ten years of watching characters on *The Bugs Bunny Show* (who I admired and revered), singing 'On With The Show This Is It.'

I have always respected cartoon characters more than people, partly because they get up and go again even after a falling anvil lands on their head.

Kenny showed me the movie when he finished editing it. The thing made no sense to me, but I liked that he had spliced in lots of footage of airplane bomb-bay doors opening and bombs raining down through the sky. He had no title for it at the time, and I don't know if he ever gave it one. I don't know what became of it, but I'd enjoy seeing it again after all these years.

I seem to recall that he edited out my ad-libbed

stunning crash. A pity... after I'd spent all those childhood years rehearsing for it.

My brilliant career as Movie-Star-Without-Pay ended when Kenny called "cut" on the last day of shooting. I had enjoyed glimpsing that strange occupation, but I could feel my born-to-it vocation (Professional Ne'er-Do-Well) calling me back.

Kenny and I lost touch. He went to New York, where I heard he attempted stand-up comedy, and to Hollywood, where I heard he directed Grease 3, and finally to Toronto, where he found big-time success at last. He is now rich and famous in Canada – producing, writing, directing and acting in big-budget national CBC television programs.

And with the way things have turned out, one may wonder... should I be retro-actively paid for all that dedication, pain and suffering so long ago?

It may well be argued that I entered into the job fully agreeing to be paid nothing, and got what I had bargained for. But would I then be justified in presenting the "Simpsonian" or "Homerian" counter-argument: "An older boy made me do it"?

I don't know the answers to these complex questions, but I do know that if you ever read this Kenny, if nothing else, it would be kind of you to mail me a harmonica holder... or a bicycle tire pressure gauge... or a decent mattress. Some things are hard to come by here on the remote Island of St. Helena.

Chapter Ten

Mr. Potato Head's Big Idea

The Island of St. Helena is far from being self-sufficient. Here, we are dependent on The Big World for so many things. And we're dependent on the one and only ship to bring the things to the island.

In this situation, it's not surprising that there are frequent shortages on the island. Things like onions, potatoes, and fresh fruit are chronically unavailable. Then the ship arrives and there is plenty – briefly.

Life is an ongoing cycle of boom-and-bust. I kind of like it. It gives you an appreciation for *stuff*. This appreciation has been lost in the endless avalanche of products and bloated consumerism in The Big World. But the boom-and-bust cycle here isn't instantly obvious. You have to be here awhile to see the pattern.

There was a family that moved here from South Africa a few years ago. They never really understood the place and they didn't stay. But they were public-spirited and thought they'd share what they knew, by writing a sort of "Handy Household Hints From Heloise" type of column in the local newspaper. An item in an early column made me laugh out loud:

> To keep your car's windscreen clear of
> the dirt from dried-up raindrops, try
> smearing it with a peeled potato.

They obviously had no concept of the value of a potato on St. Helena. I was tempted to write my own handy household hint in the next week's paper. Something a little more relevant to local reality.

> When faced with the next island-wide
> potato shortage, try licking a car
> windscreen.

Chapter Eleven

The Patron Saint of Fishcakes

Nowadays St. Helena is officially classified as a British Overseas Territory, whereas "in the before days," (as the Saints say) it was a British Colony. But no matter what title is given to the island's relationship with the UK, the bond has always been a strong one.

The Saints, many of whom have never been to England, are very British. They drink tea, they play cricket, and they drive on the wrong side of the road. A car in St. Helena does not have fenders, or a hood, or a trunk, or a horn. Cars here have wings, bonnets, boots and hooters.

Saints cling to a Britishness that has all but vanished in Britain. For example, with Victorian respect they hang pictures of The Royals on their walls. Having had no exposure to the relatively modern British trend toward Royal-mocking (as evidenced in the TV show *Spitting Image* and Sue Townsend's Royal-razzing novel *The Queen And I*) the Saints remain touchingly, and antiquatedly, Royal-loyal.

So although the St. Helena gene-pool gumbo has ingredients from Africa, Madagascar, China, Scotland, India and Java, (as well as others), the overriding flavour is unmistakably British.

There is one area however, in which the Saints do not copy their distant countrymen. Mercifully, they do not replicate British cuisine.

My most vivid memory of English cooking is of a breakfast I purchased one morning somewhere in London. I had been walking around for some time, hungrily looking for a modest restaurant. Finally I saw such a place on an out-of-the-way side street and hurried in. The café was small and crowded, which I took as a good sign. The patrons were ordinary people, just breakfasting, reading the newspaper and getting on with another day.

I quickly studied the setup: pick up tray, self-serve tea or coffee, place order with cook, pay cashier, sit down and waitress brings food. I scanned the wall-mounted menu and got in line (sorry, "queue"). When I spoke, to order two fried eggs and toast, I was conscious of the staff and patrons scrutinizing me, as if to say "we don't often get Yanks in here." The reception was neither friendly nor hostile; just observational.

I sat at a tiny table beside the window, drinking coffee. The waitress brought over my plate and set it down. She looked at me deadpan, and went off to get her next order. I looked at breakfast. The two eggs were just barely visible, submerged below the surface of a sickening swamp of dark brown congealing grease. The toast sat perched at the edge of the bog, partly submerged in the ooze. My breakfast strongly resembled a graphic example of toxic industrial waste.

My first thought was that this must be some sort of anti-Yank prank. So I looked around at the plates on other tables. I was both relieved and amazed to see that other diners had been served the same swill, and that they were behaving as if nothing weird was going on. They were eating this sludge.

I looked at it again. Very unappetizing, even when hungry. The bright red plastic tomato-shaped ketchup dispenser on the table seemed to suggest that ketchup might help. So I picked it up and had just begun squeezing it, when at that very moment there was a car accident on the street right outside the window. The noise startled me and I looked out. It was just a little fender-bender (sorry, "wing-ding"). Nothing serious, so I returned my attention to the alleged breakfast.

I thought I'd been squeezing ketchup while distracted, but I couldn't see any on the plate. I gave a test-squeeze and watched in fascinated horror as a big blob of ketchup squirted out, hit the stagnant quagmire of dark brown grease, and sank sadly out of sight, vanishing without a trace.

So I was very pleased to find the Saints not imitating British cuisine. Saints do not fry or boil their food until it tastes like either bland grease or bland mush. The Saints like to spice it hot with lots of "bite," as they call it.

And that's how it was at Dot's café.

Sadly, Dot has passed away. But the memory of her lives on in the hearts of many. Dot was locally famous for being an outstanding cook and an outspoken wild card. Her café was a mainstay for the people in Jamestown.

At Dot's café there was no menu. Her customers didn't need a menu. It was *all* good! Each weekday she would make a huge pot of something seriously delicious, such as curried tuna mince or wahoo – always caught fresh that morning. And in addition to what was in the pot, Dot would always create her unrivalled masterpiece: fishcakes! They came in two styles: "*with* bite," recommended only for the fireproof palate, and "*without* bite," meaning merely spicy-hot and zingy – popular with those of us who are flammable.

With irresistible friendliness Dot welcomed one and all to her café. She loved to laugh and to make people laugh, and she was never stuck for a funny story. Her café was island headquarters for "the walking newspaper," as she called it, and the island's latest news, gossip and rumours were exchanged across the tables.

It was only natural to find the most relaxed, most likeable down-home restaurant in the whole world here on St. Helena. Mynah birds, magnetized by the tantalizing fragrance of Dot's cooking, would climb through holes in the rusted chicken-wire-covered windows and Dot would enlist customer assistance in shooing them out.

Very few tourists realized that Dot's café existed,

since it was tucked away in the attic of a cast-iron prefab building (shipped out to St. Helena from England in 1865) and Dot had no sign outside indicating that there was a restaurant upstairs. But at the time this was pretty much standard business practice on St. Helena. Just a door. No sign. Inside might be a hardware or a grocery or a tea shop or somebody's living room.

One day, as I watched a tourist couple pass by on the street below, I asked Dot why she had no sign outside.

"Oh I'd *love* one nice sign, dollin' ...but I not got one."

So Cynthia and I offered to make Dot a sign – one with her picture on it.

Dot rummaged in a kitchen drawer and found a photo of her and her family. In it, she was all dressed up and every hair was in place – a complete contrast to her untamed appearance in the hot, busy café. Cynthia, who is an excellent portrait artist, worked her magic and managed to capture perfectly the warmth, the loving bawdy sense of humour, and the saucy spirit and soul of her subject.

We mounted the portrait on a sign that said "Dot's Café – Upstairs" and carried it, covered with a towel, into the café early one morning. Dot came out of the kitchen and we unveiled it.

I have never seen any piece of art affect anyone so strongly. Dot jumped back a step with a delighted squeal and pulled her apron up over her eyes, overwhelmed. When she could handle another peek, she peeked at it again, like a child. She just beamed. She couldn't believe it! She would have one of the few signs in town, and the *only* one with a face on it – *her* face!

But Dot didn't want to put it up outside where *she* couldn't see it.

So she kept it inside the restaurant.

She showed it to all her customers with great pride, engaging them in long conversations about how she really can *so* look that good and bringing out the family photo as proof. Eventually everyone would agree that it *was* her face, but that they'd just never seen her looking so spiffy.

Dot was so taken by the portrait, that Cynthia and I thought up another use for it. We photocopied it, and then shrunk the copy until it was the same size as the Queen of England on the St. Helena five-pound note. Then we taped the cut-out of Dot over the Queen and photocopied the bill. We made a few of the five-pound notes and gave them to Dot. Needless to say, she loved them.

We sat in the café and watched the same scene repeated with different customers. The customer would pay Dot for the meal. A mischievous glint in Dot's eye showed how much she was gleefully anticipating the big moment:

"Your change luvvy!" And she hands out the bogus fiver.

Hilarious disbelief! The customer and Dot would

convulse with laughter. A second look at the irreverent Queen Dot cash would send them both off again. When finally able to speak, the customer would ask something like, "You just Queen of St. Helena or you Queen of England too?"

Dot would say, "I just the cook now dollin, but that my next job!" and they'd sail off whooping again. The joy of Royal-mocking had finally arrived at this remote, enduring fragment of the British Empire.

*   *   *

Certain tables at Dot's were reserved each noon for her longtime, regular customers, but no signs indicated which tables were reserved. So, if a customer sat unwittingly at an unmarked reserved table, Dot would call out cheerfully from the kitchen.

"Sorry dollin, that table reserve for Mrs. So-and-so."

The customer would move, sometimes to a different unmarked reserved table, and Dot would again have to interrupt work on a culinary masterpiece to play maitre d'.

To me, this looked like another job for that Big World invention, the *sign*. So Cynthia and I came up with signs that said, "Sorry dollin, this table is reserved." They had a miniaturized version of Dot's portrait on them. There were usually only two or three reserved tables, but we made about a dozen signs, anticipating wear and tear and souvenir-hunters.

I shouldn't have been surprised, but I was, when Dot,

thrilled by her miniature portraits, put one on each table.

Customers would arrive, see that all the tables were reserved, stand around for a while, and eventually just shrug and sit down somewhere. If they happened to sit at a *genuinely* reserved table, Dot would call out cheerfully from the kitchen.

"Sorry dollin, that table reserve for Mrs. So-and-So!"

And this demented ritual just became part of the fun. An entertaining prelude to the delectable St. Helenian cooking served up by its uncontested very best practitioner: Dot Leo.

Dot Leo – The Patron Saint of Fishcakes
drawing by Cynthia Barefoot

Chapter Twelve

Off The Map

Occasionally, a passing yacht will volunteer to carry mail up to Ascension Island, 700 miles away, where there's a military airport. From there, mail is air-freighted to the UK and then beyond.

But mail usually leaves St. Helena on the RMS *St. Helena* – the last Royal Mail Ship in the world. The ship comes and goes on a variable schedule. Sometimes it sails to Ascension, sometimes to Cape Town, sometimes to England and sometimes (rarely), to the island of Tristan da Cunha (the most remote inhabited island on earth). The voyage to Ascension and back is considered a "shuttle" and usually takes only five days. The other voyages render the island ship-less and stranded – no way on or off – for periods of up to five weeks. But there's always a date and a time – a *deadline* – when overseas mail is due. As a result, the simple act of writing a friendly letter is much different here than it is in The Big World, with its daily pick-up and delivery convenience.

Letter writing here mutates within the mind, from a pleasant exchange with someone you care about, into a game-show type task that must be completed before the clock winds down and the buzzer goes.

As time elapses it gets worse; all the fun goes out of it,

and it mutates again. Now it has the unforgettable toxic flavour of an essay due at school. You casually dread it. More time evaporates. Then time starts getting *really* tight. By now you loathe it, so you find all kinds of stuff that has to be done *right now*. (Too bad I have to mystify the cats tonight by holding up the hand mirror in front of them – otherwise I could get a start on that darned letter!) Then, at the very last minute, you panic and scrawl some unintelligible gibberish on the back of a shopping list and stuff it into an envelope and hand it in at the Post Office just as it's closing, hoping you luck out and get a "D."

And these letters are what people have to go on when they think about you. You can see how easy it is to inadvertently create a false impression of mental slippage. It's also very easy to miss the deadline, which means it will be many months before anyone gets a letter from you.

Hank, my friend and fellow former lab-rat, writes to us from Winnipeg:

Dear Rex and Cynthia,
You don't write. You don't call. But enough about you.
I blah, blah, blah...

So I scribble back to him, in my customary, frantic, truncated prose:

Dear Hank,
Enough about you. I blah, blah, blah...

From this you may have gathered that we *do* get mail

on St. Helena. Eventually. Sometimes.

Part of the excitement of getting a dog-eared letter or a vandalized package is looking at all the interesting things that have been stamped all over its remains: "MIS-SENT TO ICELAND" or "MIS-DIRECTED: PROCESSED IN VENEZUELA" and so on. I'm not being sarcastic here. I'm grateful for the international mail service. It's a bridge to loved ones. Even if it is a shakey bridge.

*   *   *

All her life my Mum has won people over by love-bombing them with a surreal level of niceness. In her eighty-odd years of life, I think you could count on one hand the number of times *she's* been sarcastic.

A few years ago, as a present, she gave Cynthia and I a year's subscription to *National Geographic Magazine*. And once, the magazine actually arrived at the Post Office in Jamestown.

But that was it. No more.

Over the phone and in letters, my Mum would ask me for an update on the status of our paid for but un-delivered present. I didn't want her to have to bother with it, but I couldn't lie. Not to her. It's just not done. She's waaay too nice. So I'd have to tell her, "No *National Geographics* yet."

So my Mum phoned the magazine's subscription office, and very nicely explained that the magazines of the subscription that she'd given as a gift had failed to arrive at St. Helena. And the subscription woman assured her that it would be looked into and rectified.

But no magazines came.

More phone calls to the subscription desk – my Mum, always nice; the magazine office, always pleasant, business-like.

But no magazines.

So my Mum writes them a letter. Pleasant, but earnest. She tells them the (amazing) number of years she's been a faithful customer, and how many subscriptions she's bought over the years for people as gifts, and politely asks if they will *please* send the magazines to St. Helena.

No magazines.

So she phones the subscription desk *one last time.* And politely explains. Again, they'll look into it and blah blah blah.

MY MUM: "Well perhaps the problem is that you don't know where the Island of St. Helena *is. By any chance, do you have a map of the world over there?* Because *if you do*, get it out and have a real good look. St. Helena is a little dot in the South Atlantic Ocean. That's the ocean between Africa and South America. Is this helping you?"

But maybe the folks over at National Geographic Magazine shouldn't feel too bad. Some maps of the world don't have St. Helena on them. Like the one I was looking at in Jamestown the other day. On the wall of The Education Office.

Chapter Thirteen

The Groovy Green Donut of Inner Space

A few nights ago I woke up in the middle of the night and couldn't get back to sleep. This happens to me quite often, and usually I don't mind. Usually I'm content to just lie there and think "duh." But the other night I felt *restless*. As if there was something I ought to *do*. This was strange. Because there *is* very little to do by yourself in the middle of the night in a dark house out in the country on a small island way out in the middle of a huge ocean. But I just couldn't get back to sleep and I couldn't just lie there in bed.

So I got up and tuned in the BBC International Service on the solar-rechargeable battery-powered radio in the kitchen. Wearing the headphones so as not to wake Cynthia, I sat in the dark in my underwear and listened.

At the moment I tuned in, they announced the content of the upcoming programme – an interview with a Swiss professor who was a pioneer in chemical research and who had just turned one hundred years old. He was also the author of a book called *My Problem Child – LSD*.

I found the interview with the spry-sounding professor most interesting.

He told how in Switzerland, in 1943, while doing research into cardiovascular drugs he'd accidentally concocted a brand new substance. Then he started feeling funny. He locked up the lab and went home, where he lay on the couch and had a strange and marvellous time. The next day he tried to analyze his odd experience, and decided it must have resulted from getting some of the new molecules on his hands. So he ingested some on purpose – and survived – after living through a technicolour nightmare. Further experimentation showed him that after taking very minute doses he had hugely wonderful, exhilarating experiences... but if the dose got too high, existence became a terrifying ordeal.

The professor said that he'd always thought his creation had great potential to benefit the human race. Then he lamented how it had escaped from the lab to become a wildly uncontrolled "street drug" during the late sixties. He was dismayed that LSD had since been outlawed, and was currently campaigning to have the legislation changed. He thought it still might some day prove to be a useful therapeutic tool in the treatment of some mental conditions, such as severe autism.

When the interview ended I turned the radio off and sat quietly in the darkness.

There was much to think about.

Like how scientists with the best of intentions cannot possibly ever know whether their work will ultimately benefit or harm humankind. And how one man might look at something and see a useful tool for helping the less fortunate among us, while another man can look at the exact same thing and see a powerful weapon for frying enemy minds... and yet another man looks at it and sees a golden opportunity to make himself even crazier than he already is...

Soon the whole topic had me in a reverie, travelling backward through time. Back to the oddness known as the 1970s. I recalled that I was in desperate financial straits when I heard of an opportunity through my weird friend Henry, who I shall call "Hank" in order to protect his identity.

At that time in history, it was fashionable for the American CIA to secretly fund bizarre experiments in Canada. It is probable that the CIA were testing a new cold war weapon when they secretly funded the feeding of LSD to unsuspecting mental patients in a Montreal sanatorium. In the aftermath of that (predictably) disastrous experiment, the CIA adopted a new strategy. They began a program of secretly funding "studies" at Canadian universities. The CIA gave the universities "grants" (anonymously), and the universities hired students as guinea pigs.

Although it may sound strange to us today, back then the CIA had arrived at the conclusion that university students are a more stable group than institutionalized mental patients.

And so it came about that Hank arrived at my rent-due apartment one wintry day to announce that the University of Manitoba Psychology Department was offering one hundred dollars per person for those who could endure a week of total sight deprivation. It should be noted that money was worth much more back in The Olden Days.

According to Hank, all you had to do for the hundred bucks was to stay inside a room, blindfolded for a week, while psychology students watched you through one-way glass. Hank's problem was that the experiment called for two fishes in the fishbowl. He needed a fellow lab-rat.

Of course, it is the self-sworn duty of the Professional Ne'er-Do-Well to go wherever the weirdness wants you to be, and being a thorough Professional, I signed on.

Hank had obtained a list of the do's and don'ts of the job. It read as follows:

Subjects must wear the sight deprivation apparatus at all times. Removal of the apparatus, even momentarily, will result in immediate expulsion from the experiment.

Subjects are required to get up each day at eight A.M. and to eat breakfast.

Subjects must eat lunch at twelve noon and dinner at five P.M. each day.

Wake-up and meal consumption are mandatory (no uninterrupted sleeping all day).

Subjects must eat the food provided, with

the exception that on the seventh night it is permissible to have a staff member phone out for a pizza.

Subjects are free to quit the experiment any time they choose. The amounts payable to those staying less than the full term are as follows:

> Subjects staying less than three days and three nights will receive no pay

> Subjects staying four days and four nights will be paid fifteen dollars.

> Subjects staying five days and five nights will be paid thirty-five dollars.

> Subjects staying six days and six nights will be paid sixty dollars.

> Subjects staying seven days and seven nights will be paid one hundred dollars.

Subjects are permitted to listen to music (bring a radio if desired).

Looking over the list I felt confident that I could go the course, with the possible exception of listening to the radio.

At that time the blight of disco music was newly arrived and it blanketed the airwaves of the world. I worried that an entire week of electronic drum beats, computer-generated bass lines, vacuous lyrics, and synthetic soul was a torture under which I might crack. I confessed my fear to Hank, who suggested that he bring along his record player. Aware that Hank was capable of somewhat deviant and dreadful tastes in music I hesitantly agreed, on the condition that I could also bring some records with me.

I didn't own any records, but I thought I could possibly borrow some from my brother, who had an excellent collection. My brother, Robert, who I shall call "Bob" in order to protect his identity, always had the very latest Dylan, Stones, and Neil Young albums. Often when visiting him I would see a new album and ask to hear it. If he agreed to honour my musical request, Bob's Unwritten Law came into effect: He *and only he*, would actually *touch* the record or the stereo (although we commoners were permitted to watch). Bob would reverently and expertly remove the record from the dust jacket, touching only the thin edges of the disc. He would set the record on the turntable with the calm and careful determination of a bomb-disposal expert. Then, with surgical finesse he would micro-adjust many dials and press certain selected buttons. To Bob, playing a pressed vinyl recording on high fidelity audio equipment was a Very Serious Operation Indeed.

So when I casually asked to borrow a few albums for a week or so I carefully neglected to mention that I would be newly-blind while playing them. And after lengthy, in-depth, agonizing negotiations, I finally emerged triumphant, armed with several discs.

On the appointed day, Hank and I presented ourselves promptly at eight a.m. to an office on the fourth floor of the Psychology Building on the sprawling University of Manitoba campus. The professor running the experiment was surprised that Hank had brought a record player and a big shopping bag full of records. He seemed relieved that Hank also brought a radio. We each had a sleeping bag and I carried my few borrowed albums under my arm.

We filled in some forms, giving basic information (age, sex, education, etc.). Then the professor showed us the Observation Lab. It was a small, beige, clinical room starkly furnished with only a table and several folding chairs. On the opposite wall was a door and a large darkened window. The professor flipped a light switch and an adjoining room became brightly visible through the one-way glass. The fluorescently-lit Isolation Room was also small, beige, bare and clinical, containing only a small couch and two foam mats on the floor.

"That's where you'll be staying and in here is where you'll eat your meals," said our host matter-of-factly. "You'll be buzzed on the intercom at quarter to eight each morning. Then at eight the door will be opened and you'll be led out to eat at this table. All meals are half an hour. Then you'll be led back into the Isolation Room. There'll be someone in here twenty-four hours a day. When you want to go to the bathroom you buzz the observer in this room by intercom and they'll lead you to the washroom, which is down the hall. All right so far?"

This was asked tauntingly, in an are-you-chicken-yet type of tone.

Realizing that the professor had not yet spotted that we were thoroughly professional Professionals, we began his education by offering "taint nuthin" shrugs.

The professor perceived our tough-stuff approach and responded. He upped the tension by saying in an ominous, serious tone, "Before I blindfold you, I perform a little test first. Come this way."

He set off briskly down the hall, giving Hank and I a chance to exchange chicken-filled glances.

But we dutifully followed the professor down the hall and into an office. Inside there were two chairs on opposite sides of a table. On the table stood a vertical white panel, about three feet high and three feet long with a six-inch round hole in the middle of it. Also on the table was a glass jar of what looked like black paint with a small paint brush beside it, and a set of about twenty glass rods, each about six inches long.

After giving us a few seconds to eyeball the apparatus, the professor spoke.

"I need you one at a time for this. One of you wait in the hall. Who's first?"

Hank ended up in the hall and the professor closed the door.

"Sit down," he said, "and I'll explain what we're going to do."

I sat.

"You'll roll up your sleeve and I'll paint a small circle of this black ink on the inside of your forearm. It's completely washable and there's nothing to worry about. Then you'll put your arm through this hole, palm up," (he indicated the hole in the white card standing on the table) "and I'll tickle your arm at the black spot with the hairs on these rods."

He held up a glass rod and I could now see that a single hair protruded out of the end of the rod.

"These rods are numbered and each one has a finer hair attached to it. You'll tell me when you feel the hair tickling your arm. You just say 'now' whenever you feel the tickle. We'll repeat this after you've been blindfolded for a week to see if you've improved. OK?"

I nodded my understanding and we proceeded. I could hear the professor's pen moving as he recorded the results on the other side of the little white wall. We finished in about ten minutes. The professor seemed friendlier and more respectful as he thanked me and asked me to send Hank in.

Out in the hall I motioned for Hank to go in. He gave an inquiring look and I answered with another "taint nuthin" shrug.

When Hank was done we carried our belongings into the Isolation Room. We plugged in the record player and the radio and set the albums down in two stacks on the floor, Hank's stack dwarfing my few discs. After unrolling our sleeping bags on the foam mats on the floor we heard the intercom buzz and then the professor's voice.

"All right, fellas. Come into the Observation Lab and I'll put on the blindfolds and we can get started."

The blindfold was a thick black cloth bag that went right over my head. There was a small cut-out for the mouth and a peaked nose with a small triangular cut-out for the nostrils. As soon as the bag went over my head the blackness was total and absolute. The professor tightened some straps at my neck and asked, "Are you all right? Can you breathe?"

I replied that yes, I could; I was all right. Then I heard him blindfolding Hank and asking him the same questions. Hank sounded unruffled when he replied, "Yeah."

"All right then. I'll lead you in now."

After leading us in the professor said, "If you want anything, buzz on the intercom and someone will answer."

Then we heard the door shut.

DAY ONE:

We bumbled around until we found the couch and sat down. We discussed at great length the discomfort of having cloth bags over our heads and whether or not we could handle an entire week of it. Gradually I became aware that I was watching tiny floating light particles moving around in the blackness. I asked Hank if he also saw them. He said he did, and that they were the normal after-images that everyone sees when you close your eyes. This sounded right to me.

Before long the intercom buzzed and we heard an announcement. It wasn't the professor's voice. It was a singsong mischievous-sounding male voice. It sounded as if he knew a joke that we didn't.

♪ "Lunchtime, guys." ♫

We heard the door open. We were led by the hand out to the Observation Lab and seated at the table.

"There's two sandwiches on a plate in front of each of you, and I'll pour you both a coffee. How do you take it?" asked the owner of the mischievous voice.

We gave our answers. I heard the coffee being poured and an unseen hand guided mine to the cup. I fumbled my other hand forward and found the plate of sandwiches. Our "caretaker" was standing by and somehow I could sense him giving off an energy of gleeful malicious anticipation. Reluctantly, I picked up a sandwich and took a bite. It was absolutely revolting.

"What *is* this?" I gasped, gagging.

"That? Oh, it's Klik," he answered in a tone of mock innocence, as if to say, "Gosh! Didn't anyone mention this?" He snickered delightedly when I moaned.

For those of you who are fortunate enough to be unfamiliar with Klik: It is alleged to be a canned luncheon "meat." It is composed of the various unmentionable body parts (and their various unmentionable secretions) of various unmentionable animals, mingled with lotsa Tantalizing Test-Tube Flavour. The good folks over at Klik pack each lump in its very own blob of greasy gelatin. The composition and source of the jelly-blob is a closely guarded trade secret, but rumours persist that somehow Roto-Rooter (the guys that suck the slime from clogged drain pipes) is involved.

Remembering that meal consumption was a necessary step toward getting paid, I (a Professional) swallowed hard and followed with a coffee chaser. I have been a vegetarian for over three decades now.

Boldly, I ate my entire lunch and soon Hank and I were led back into the Isolation Room. We sat on the couch and became absorbed in watching the now-intensifying light show. At times, the lights seemed to pulse orange-red in waves. Then the waves would dissolve into pale yellow-green islands drifting through the inky black. The islands would shatter into millions of floating specks, all in a random pattern of change.

For a while, we described what we were seeing to each other. Then we created a game in which one of us would get up and try to walk around the room. It surprised us both to find out how disoriented we were.

We both found it hysterically funny to be sitting safely on the couch listening to the other guy stumble and smash his head on the cement-block wall. Soon we had large goose-eggs rising on our heads. I like to think we tired of this entertainment this side of permanent brain damage.

We returned to "tripping" safely on the couch for a while. Then Hank got up. And the real trouble began. I heard Hank bumble around a bit. Then a click... some shuffling sounds... zzziip! ...followed by the unmistakable voice of *Barbara Streisand* wailing some god-awful schmaltz and Hank cheering ecstatically, "Babs! BAAABS!"

I tried valiantly to block the horrendous audio assault, but the cornball vibrato wailing and Hank's adoring cheering easily penetrated the muffle of my hands and the bag over my ears. I tried kneeling on the floor and stuffing my head inside the couch cushions. I was dimly aware that third-year psychology students in the Observation Lab were watching and would likely be taking notes:

2:17 p.m. - Subject A exhibiting apparent Ostrich Syndrome in response to aural stimuli. (head stuffed in couch)

The vile howling completely invaded my head. I emerged from the couch cushions and emphatically instructed Hank to put an immediate halt to the uncalled-for audio violence. Hank's only response was to sing along to the record at the top of his lungs, perversely revelling in the fact that he *ACTUALLY KNEW THE WORDS* to this wretched crap.

2:21 p.m. - Subject B yelling song lyrics; possible fear-response mechanism. (an extreme form of whistling in the dark?)

I had tried peaceable means. This was war.

I stood up and headed straight for the record player. Almost immediately I smashed forcefully into a wall and sank to my knees. Over and above Hank's and Babs' caterwauling I thought I detected the sound of cruel hysterical laughter seeping through the Observation Lab's glass wall.

I remember that a brief out-of-body experience followed, in which I floated up and saw myself, crumpled in a heap on the floor. There was a cartoon balloon floating above my black-bagged head and I could clearly read the words written in it:

" C...CAN'T...TAKE SCHM... SCHMALTZ!
MMM...MUST...STOP... RECORD !! "

I was suddenly conscious of being back inside my body with my hands touching the obvious contours of the record player. I grabbed desperately for the needle and was rewarded. ZZZZZIIIP! At last, merciful silence from Babs, leaving only Hank, momentarily unaware of the loss of his partner in this savage duet, ranting high volume solo. Hank stopped "singing" when he realized what had happened.

"Hey! What happened to Babs? You bastard!"

I deftly switched tactics from direct action to diplomacy. I suggested to Hank that although Babs Music is undeniably terrific, it is not good music to *trip* to... and that I could put on some beats more appropriate to the light show. Maybe the Stones. (Here again I thought I detected muffled snickering coming through the wall.)

Although crazy, Hank prides himself on being open-minded and adventurous, and eventually he agreed to give it a try. I succeeded in extracting the offending Babs from the turntable and felt around for the record jacket to put it away. Waves of panic and horror pulsed through me as I absorbed the shocking reality of what had happened: The records were no longer in two neat piles. They had become hopelessly messed around during our disorientation game! I could hear the nervous edginess in my voice as I blurted out the sordid facts of our situation to Hank – who seemed unable to grasp the seriousness of it.

Sweating and praying, I clumsily put a record on the turntable. zzzip! WAAAIL!

"BAAAABS!" Hank cheered wildly. "HAHAHAHA! GO BABS BABY, GO!"

Again he started "singing" along, somehow even louder than before.

I knew the odds were very much against me. There were only a few decent albums lost somewhere in that treacherous minefield of audio torture. Bravely, I tried first one record and then another, always with the same terrifying result: If it wasn't Babs it was Abba. I was losing round after round in a nightmare game of Audio Russian Roulette.

As the last shreds of my sanity unravelled I became wilder with the needle. And I admit there was some serious scratching, perhaps even gouging of records during my panicky search for a musical antidote to the audio toxins I had unwillingly ingested. I also must admit I wasn't overly concerned about damaging these records. I knew I was unintentionally performing A Necessary Service For Hank's Own Good.

"Hey! Watch it willya?" yelled Hank with every zzzip!

I apologized insincerely.

With only seconds to spare before my total mental meltdown, suddenly there it was – *Dylan!* Eagerly, I began absorbing this musical salve. Hank jumped up.

"THIS STUFF IS TOTAL CRUD!" he yelled.

Realizing what would come next I (blindly) lunged for him and missed completely.

Two thoughts filled my head as I heard the needle viciously mutilate an entire side of Dylan. "My brother's gonna kill me" and "I'm gonna kill Hank." And here is what I learned from the events that followed:

1. When fighting blindfolded in a small room, it is very easy to inflict as much damage on yourself as on your opponent.

2. While blindfolded, it is surprisingly easy to vandalize record albums.

3. While vandalising record albums blindfolded, it is impossible to distinguish between "friendly" and "enemy" albums.

I really don't know how the fight might have ended had we not been interrupted by the sound of the intercom buzzer, followed by the voice of someone trying to recover from a wild laughing fit."Aha!... okay... HAH! You *guys*! ahahaha!... Dinner time! HAHAHAHAHA!"

I knew that the psychology students ('psychos' we called 'em) were sniggering at us as we sat down to a delicious dinner of Klik sandwiches and coffee. But I didn't care. The brawl had given me a good appetite, and it was with gusto that I gobbled my animal offal/ CIA-Brand Hallucinogen/Roto-Rooter sandwiches.

While sitting on the couch after "dinner," I took stock of the situation. On the down side, we were covered with huge sore lumps ...and we had wrecked every record album we had brought in ...and we would be at the mercy of radio disc jockeys for the remaining six days and seven nights. But on the up side, Hank and I were evenly matched ...and the light show was really picking up ...and we had the satisfaction of having done a good day's work.

DAY TWO:

BUZZZZ! "Good morning gentlemen! Everybody up!"

I woke, and naturally, opened my eyes. Rather than the usual humdrum first-thing-in-the-morning sights, my brain was stabbed by intense abstract hallucinations. Quite disorienting. Gradually, with effort, I was able to establish and sort the relevant facts. I was blindfolded and injured and sharing a room with a dangerous, blindfolded, Babs-obsessed lunatic, whose sole mission in life was to expand the known boundaries of human insanity. We were both on a diet of unknown chemical origin. And for descending into this traumatizing nightmare netherworld I was gonna be up one hundred sweet smackaroos in less than a week. This last thought cheered me immensely.

And day two passed pleasantly enough. Paradoxically, the hallucinations seemed to distract Hank from the fact that he was crazy, and he settled in as a well-behaved, interested observer. We spent the day watching and describing lights and patterns.

We were both still feeling the physical effects of the previous day's musical difference of opinion, and there was an unspoken agreement to avoid even mentioning turning on the radio. And with all the lights, music seemed unnecessary.

Following the evening hit of Klik we watched as wriggling spermatazoa-like pinpoints of light fused into a glowing, pulsing, shimmering pale-green blob. A black pinhole would then form in the center of the blob and grow larger and larger... until the blob became a floating green gaseous-looking donut. Then the donut would shatter into millions of brilliant tiny wandering pinpoints of light and the cycle would begin again. What I found most interesting was that although we were both experiencing the same hallucination, neither of us could "will" the donut into existence; it would arrive of its own accord in its own good time.

DAY THREE:

Buzzer. Wake-up call. I opened my eyes. There it was.

"Hey Hank – see it?"

"Yup."

The Groovy Green Donut Of Inner Space hung there, pulsing and glowing eerily in the infinite blackness. As the day progressed we became aware of a new phenomenon: the donut never left. It didn't shatter or fade. It floated in front of our eyes, constantly commanding our focus with its hypnotic glow. We watched it all day, mesmerized by each pulse and soft luminous bloom within the gaseous green ring.

And days four, five and six all floated past, just like day three... just groovin' on the groovy green.

DAY SEVEN:

I had lost all sense of time. Any life that I might have lived before seemed vague and unreal, like a movie I'd heard about but hadn't seen. I felt as though I had always lived in the little room with Hank, endlessly digging the green donut and eating electric Klik. I felt very comforted by the donut's continued presence. It was like a beautiful beacon in the endless velvety blackness of deep inner space. So *cosmically* groovy!

The intercom buzzed. A respectful voice asked what kind of pizza we'd like to order. The arrival of the pizza put us both in a party mood, and by mutual consent we turned on the radio. Predictably, it spewed banal bouncing disco-flavoured pap, but I, having been toughened by my earlier encounter with audio Hell, munched away happily.

And suddenly, appearing on the aural landscape like a mirage ...like a life-giving oasis in a vast dead desert, was a brand new song by Paul McCartney, called "It's Just Another Day." It was very good. Later, I curled up in front of the donut and fell asleep with the song playing inside my head.

On the eighth morning, after the intercom's buzz, we heard the professor's voice for the first time since he led us into the Isolation room. He sounded cheerful.

"Good morning, fellas! I'll give you guys a few minutes to wake up and then I'll be in to remove the blindfolds, okay?"

Hank gave an enthusiastic "Yessir!" and I nodded reluctantly. To me, the removal of the blindfold meant the loss of the donut and a return to the outer world. I felt like a hermit being forced to attend a party.

The professor came in saying, "Well done, guys. You made it. Not everyone does y'know! Now I'm sure you're anxious to get those things off your heads, but just before we do that let me explain something. You've been cut off from all light for a week and when the blindfold comes off the light is going to hurt your eyes a bit. So I'll remove the blindfolds in this room where there's just dim light coming from the Observation Lab. I suggest you spend fifteen minutes in here before you go into the Observation Lab, and then fifteen minutes in there before going out into the hallway... just to give your eyes a chance to adjust gradually. In half an hour we'll repeat the arm-tickling test and then you get paid and you can go home. Okay?"

"Fine by me!" said the enthusiastic Hank. I nodded resignedly.

I could hear the professor undoing the straps of Hank's blindfold as I concentrated on taking one long last look at the donut. I wanted to mentally photograph it so I could remember it forever. Then Hank was exclaiming "WOW!" over and over again as the professor was undoing my blindfold.

When the bag was pulled off my head, there, in front of me, magnificent and beautiful, hung... the donut! I was euphoric.

I noticed that the donut no longer hung in the

absolute blackness. It hung in a dark room in which the dim outlines of the walls, the floor, the ceiling, and the professor and Hank were zooming away from me at high speed and zooming back up at me again. The donut floated in a fixed position as the room zoomed in and out around it. The wild and unexpected visuals were accompanied by pain in my eyes.

"Okay then, I'll see you in half an hour," said the professor. He exited through the Observation Lab into the hallway, closing the door behind him.

Silence. The Observation Lab was empty. We weren't being watched! I felt like a kid in school when the teacher steps out of the classroom. I was filled with a liberated, delinquent, what'll-we-get-up-to giddiness.

Hank asked, "Are you seeing all this?" He described the donut floating in the wildly zooming room. Then he jumped up from the couch and rushed into the Observation Lab.

"Oh wow! You gotta check this out! Wow!"

I hesitated. It had been less than five minutes since our blindfolds had come off and my eyes ached.

"C'mere! This is totally unbelievable!"

I entered the glowing Observation Lab. It was a brilliantly-coloured crazy zooming light show starring the donut. The colours were madly electric – all lit up from within. I was just beginning to comprehend this insanity when Hank opened the door to the hall. Our eyes stung fiercely. The savage brilliance of the fluorescent lights momentarily stunned us both.

"Hot damn!" said Hank.

We careened down the unworldly, glowing, elastic hallway and followed the donut out into the corridor. There, huge glowing floor-to-ceiling windows attracted us like moths to a flame. The shocking glare of the sunshine reflecting off the brilliant white snow outside quick-toasted our eyes and our brains. When we were charbroiled to perfection we zombied back to the office, where the professor repeated the tickle test.

He handed us our pay and thanked us politely. We thanked him, gathered our sleeping bags, and zoomed off into the glowing satisfaction of a good job well done.

*　　　*　　　*

EPILOGUE:

Within three days of completing the experiment, the Groovy Green Donut Of Inner Space had faded, and then vanished. The world had gradually stopped zooming in and out, and things had returned to their normal, non-electric colours.

It was not until the 1990s that investigative reporters for a Canadian television program uncovered the fact that the CIA was behind the Montreal Sanatorium LSD Disaster and the University of Manitoba Sensory Deprivation Experiments.

There were lawsuits, but I did not file. It would have

been very easy for me to blame all the failures and mistakes of my adult life on the physical, chemical and psychological damage done to me during that mission. But it wouldn't have been fair, because for every minus the experience generated, there has also been a plus. For example, I am unable to eat Klik... but on the other hand, I am unable to eat Klik.

And I should mention that the experience did not lead to damaging habitual drug abuse. Like U.S. President Bill Clinton, I engaged in nothing beyond the normal harmless youthful experimentation. So yeah, sure, maybe I dropped a little acid...
BUT I DIDN'T INHALE!

*   *   *

And so, decades later, I sit in the darkness in my kitchen on St. Helena, on a pitch black moonless night, and hum along to the music I hear playing inside my head. I do it quietly so as not to wake Cynthia. It's impossible to stop smiling as a I hum along with Barbara Streisand's beautiful voice belting out 'On A Clear Day You Can See Forever.'

Chapter Fourteen

Saint-Speak

Not all Saints speak what I'd call "Saint-speak." Some have been to England and have come back speaking "perfect BBC posh." But I think most Saints understand Saint-speak even if they don't speak it.

I find it quite difficult to decode. Cynthia's much better at it than I am.

I'm told that Saint-speak came into being during the dark days of slavery, when unfortunate people were kidnapped from far-flung places, like India's Malabar coast and Mozambique and Madagascar and Java, and shipped to this island to labour as slaves for brutal English overseers. The slaves had no language in common so they resourcefully created one, based on English, but *different* from English – probably so they could communicate amongst themselves without the slave-owner knowing what was being said.

Saint-speak is, to the modern Canadian ear, at least partly staccato gibberish. Often one syllable will stand for a three-syllable word. Sometimes syllables are compressed: "Half Tree Hollow" becomes "Awf-trolla." Add to this an unusual sort of English / South African / Australian-ish accent. Add to this the fact that fragments of Dickensian Olde English are still in use here, such as the selective switching of v's and w's – "wittles" instead of "vittles". Mystifying when it's all strung together, at speed.

"Wilma is not going to Half Tree Hollow. She doesn't have a van." becomes "Vilma not go Awftrolla – she not got one wan." The "she not got one wan" part is said as one syllable.

My usual reply to everything is just to smile while thinking, "Wha?" But if you don't try to decode Saint-speak – if you just *listen* to it – it has a really lovely lilt.

Of course, there's a flip-side to all this. The Saints find the way *we* speak weird, but exotic and funny. They have trouble with our oddball words and our slow-as-molasses Texas drawl delivery (which probably makes us seem stupid and cartooney to them). For example: I walk into a general store, crammed floor-to-ceiling with a huge range of "stuff," and ask if they sell "metal pails" (and here I hasten to point out that I *don't* pronounce "pails" as a two-syllable word: "pay-uls"). My request brings confusion to the shop-girl's face. So she calls over another clerk and (while shooting a "watch this" look at the other clerk) she says, "What you want again?"

They both lean forward. I have their full attention.

"I'm just wondering if you sell metal pails."

They look at each other, just on the edge of cartoon-character-induced giggles. They don't have a clue what I've said.

"Sorry luvvy, us not got *that*."

"Okay, thanks," and I start to walk out the door. Suddenly one of them *decodes* it.

"Wait luvvy!" Then to the other clerk: "He want one *tin bucket!*"

So I, a livin', breathin' Foghorn Leghorn, buys a tin bucket.

I think we're getting used to each other here now, but when we first came I had a series of encounters that, at the time, I didn't understand. A Saint would approach me with the standard greeting: "You alright?" I'd learned the correct response: "Not too bad." Here, if someone asks you, "You alright?" it is mandatory that you answer "Not too bad," (even if a large falling anvil has just finished landing on your head). Next, the Saint would *ask* me something such as, "So... you like it here?"

At the time, I didn't realize that for the Saint, this was like dropping a coin into a jukebox. In my ignorance I'd mistake it for an actual *question* and I'd answer, "Yes" and go on a bit about the nice weather or what a pretty island it is or how nice the people are. But then I'd move on to a meatier subject, like perhaps a recent political event, hoping to move our conversation beyond the surfacey and the trivial. I'd go into the pros and cons of a recent government decision, and what I thought the future ramifications may be for the island and how... and suddenly I'd realize that the Saint who *started* this conversation isn't tuning in. He's *listening,* yes – but his eyes have glazed over and there's an amused smile on his face. So I stop speaking.

And instead of replying, "I disagree totally," or "You're absolutely right" or something, the Saint says, "You talk like one Amaircun."

After a few of these aborted "conversations," I finally figured out what was going on. Everything I was saying – all my well-thought-out insights into the state of affairs in this curious little world – were translating into an exotic hillbilly-twanged "blah blah blah" from faraway Nashville. "Conversation" with me was just a good tune where the words don't get in the way.

Hey man, jus' keep on riffin'. I'm diggin' ya.

*   *   *

And when it's The Saints that are riffin', our best hope for decoding is Cynthia. She picked up a lot by hanging around with the neighbourhood kids. Kids are always entertained by the novelty of an adult who doesn't "get" anything, and they happily repeated things and explained things until the nice funny lady understood.

Cynthia reads to them in her exotic Canadian drawl, and they like her for that. But they also like her because she has worms.

The kids around here had never seen a Vermicomposting worm farm before and they were fascinated. The worm farm's biggest fan is our young neighbour, Cody, who at age nine has a keen interest in gardening. It isn't just interacting with hundreds of wiggling slimey lifeforms that appeals to him. He also has a gardener's appreciation for the rich black organic fertilizer that the worms create from vegetable scraps and strips of torn paper. Cody was so impressed by the worm farm that he gave Cynthia two of *his* worms – Scamp and Poison Scamp.

One day Cody came down to Barefoot Cottage proudly carrying a book that he'd gotten as an award at school. It was a picture atlas of the world, showing interesting stuff like the animals and landscapes and people and buildings of different countries. Cynthia and Cody happily sat down together and started getting into the book. When they came to the section on Canada, Cynthia told him about exotic things like snow and bears and moose and skunks, and she said that because she came from Canada she was a "Canadian."

Cody thought deeply for a minute about the strange origin of this odd but nice lady... and then suddenly asked, "Do you know how to speak English?"

Cynthia gave a surprised little laugh and said, "Yes! We're speaking English to each other right now!"

Cody looked at her sharply, *very* offended. "I not speak *English!* Us speak *SAINT!*"

Our neighbours with their "guys" on Guy Fawkes Day.
L to R: Myrell, Jordan, Cody and Weston.

Chapter Fifteen

Tiny Minds On Parade

Here on St. Helena, I've come across a twilight zone where the line between reality and cartoons is blurry. I discovered it while walking along the one and only road that goes around this end of the island. The narrow road winds in and out of little canyons and zig-zags up and down steep ravines and valleys. Very scenic.

Often the scene is completely still, no vehicle moving, no sound except the birds singing... and dogs barking in the distance.

The hypnotic rhythm of walking and the monotony of the distant barking lulls me. My mind wanders and takes me back in time and across the planet to Hank's small messy house in Winnipeg. Hank is showing me a cartoon in a magazine. We crack up. We agree that it is the funniest cartoon to ever appear in a magazine. It depicts two apartment blocks across the street from each other. Two dogs face each other from opposite 4th floor windows. Their mouths are open and they're looking crazed.

Each has a balloon coming from his mouth that says: Bark! Bark! Bark! Bark! The caption is:

"Shut up!"

"Shut up!"

"No! *You* shut up!"

"No! *You* shut up!"

I round a bend on the road. After living here for four years the pretty-as-a-picture landscape can still grab me. So it does, and suddenly I'm back, still walking and brainlessly listening to the barking.

Then it occurs to me to wonder, "What *are* they barking at? Can't be me – I'm still a few S-curves away. They don't know I'm here."

I keep walking, following the road. The barking gets louder and louder, until I round a bend, and there, in the yard of an isolated house, stands a dog, barking frantically at the sky in a lathered fit. He is so busy and so pissed off that he barely registers that I'm there. I stop to observe. I listen. Then I understand. He is barking at a perfect, crystal-clear echo.

"Shut up!"

"Shut up!"

"No! *You* shut up!"

"No! *You* shut up!"

"No! *You* shut up!"

"No! *You* shut up!"

"No! *You* shut up!"

"No! *You* shut up!"

"No! *You* shut up!"

"No! *You* shut up!"

"No! *You* shut up!"

"No! *You* shut up!"

Chapter Sixteen

A Scholarly Treatise on the Endemic Flora and Fauna of the Island of St. Helena

There are plants and creatures on St. Helena that cannot be found anywhere else in the whole world.

This of course fascinates certain bespectacled nerds who obsess on such things. ("Look Blanche! The rare endemic Bastard Gumwood – *Commidendrum Rotundifolium!*") People who actually *have* a life are generally bored comatose by this stuff.

But *everyone* sits up and takes notice when you casually mention that St. Helena is the only place on Planet Earth to have spawned ...The Giant Earwigs.*

Today, the Giant Earwig (*Labidura herculeana*) – THE WORLD'S LARGEST EARWIG – is classified as endangered, but it is thought by some to be extinct. It was rediscovered in 1965-67, and has not been found live since. But the island has a habit of hiding supposedly vanished endemic species for years, and then one day somebody finds a small colony, or an individual, living in some almost inaccessible crevice or cave in a remote cliff somewhere.

So whenever I'm out walking, I keep a sharp lookout.

I always spin around very quickly every few steps,

*not entirely true; Wawa, Ontario spawned a rock band of that name in 1965 hoping to get the drop on one of these Supposedly Vanished Giant Earwigs. Although I haven't actually encountered one yet, I'm willing to bet that your best defense is going to be the element of surprise.

You see, the Giant Earwig assumes that because you think of it as "extinct," it can silently slime up behind unsuspecting you on a lonely deserted coastal path, and POUNCE – coiling its tentacle-like body round and round you and squeezing mercilessly until your brains come vomiting out your ear-holes.

Now, I admit I'm no Giant Earwig-*ologist* or anything (although I *have* studied boys' trashy adventure comic books). But you don't need no University-level book-learnin' to know that "Giant" is a scientific techno-term for "scary." So even if we overlook the creepy "earwig" aspect of this *thing*, common sense tells us not only to be afraid – but to be very, *very* afraid. (To avoid charges of fear-mongering, I won't even mention the large pinchers protruding from the beast's bum area) (or "bummal area" if you prefer scientific terminology).

But just as sure as there's a Giant Earwig lurking in some remote cave on St. Helena today, waking up from a long extinction-faking nap and starting to think about a freshly-squeezed tourist-brain breakfast... there's *also* bound to be some fact-obsessed science-nerd who'll read this and start complaining that I haven't a *clue* as to what I'm talking about. He or she will be quick to point out that the Giant Earwig, even when it *wasn't* extinct, was less than four inches long. Tops. And that it was harmless. They'll probably even claim that the name "Giant" was all just a big mistake, made by a near-sighted fellow-science-nerd whose observations were distorted by a new pair of thick spectacles.

Then they'll probably go on about how biodiversity and St. Helena's endemic species *are* important and interesting. They're bound to mention that *Charles Darwin* found such things interesting. And that when *he* visited St. Helena in 1836, he noted that of the 746 types of plants on the island, fifty-two were indigenous species.

And no doubt they'll say that the Wirebird, (*Charadrius Sanctaehelae*) is interesting, if only because there are just two hundred to four hundred left on earth – all on St. Helena of course.

But I doubt I'd take too much flak if I bad-mouthed St. Helena's Spiky Yellow Woodlouse (*Laureola atlantica*) because although it's a rare endemic, even science-nerds have to be just a *little* ashamed of going ga-ga over something that is after all, a *louse*.

Now don't get me wrong. Just because I'm not wild about lice and don't relish the thought of having my brains projectile-vomited from my ears... and just because I don't want to cozy up to something GIANT, that has menacing *pinchers* ON ITS BUM (which I won't even mention) ...it doesn't mean I don't care about ecology.

I do.

I recognize the global importance of St. Helena's unique biodiversity. I *understand* the significance of the fact that the island is a refuge not only for locally evolved endemic species, but for lifeforms that colonized St. Helena ten million years ago and have since disappeared from the rest of the planet.

In other words, I *care* about the beautiful tree fern (*Dicksonia arborescens*) which "has been on St. Helena for at least nine million years but no longer occurs in its likely source area of Africa" (www.worldwildlife.org). And I was saddened to learn that the last wild tree of the St. Helena Olive died in 1994. Just another casualty of humankind's five-hundred-year rampage of eco-destruction in the island's fourteen *million* year history. It disturbs me that, according to the World Wildlife web site, "over half of the plants described in 1875 have since disappeared from the island" and that of four endemic landbird species that existed on the island when humans arrived – a cuckoo, two flightless rails and a hoopoe – all we have left is a few fossils.

So I applaud the islanders and the imported scientists who are trying to rescue St. Helena's lost terrestrial eco-regions. A serious effort is being made to reverse the loss of ancient tree-fern thicket in Diana's Peak National Park. And a wide range of exotic species have been planted in the 109.5 acres of Plantation Forest. The establishment of the Millennium Gumwood Forest was an island-wide effort involving the planting of thousands of rare gumwood trees. And with the George Benjamin Arboretum, the Casons Nature Walk, the Clifford Arboretum, and the St. Helena Nature Conservation Group walks, hikers can now experience a dazzling display of unique biodiversity – Cape Yew trees, the Chinese Fir, the Norfolk Pine, the Monterey Cypress, indigenous ferns and the Silky Oak to name just a very few.

I really do care about the island's rare endemics and its biodiversity.

You can see I do.

But I question the concept of conserving *everything*. For example, saving the He Cabbage Tree and the She Cabbage Tree, and the Blushing Snail seems to me like a good idea. But who in their right mind wants to save something called "The Dwarf Jellico?" (*Sium burchellii*) I mean, come *on!* "*Jell*-i-i-ick-o?" It's *obviously* a dangerous offshoot of The Blob That Ate Chicago (*Ickia jellyus late movieum*). Dwarf *now*, sure. But just conserve it and give it time: "*Help Lance! Help!* The GIANT Jellico! It's *gaining* on me! AAAAAAAAAAAGHH!"

I'm sure there's going to be objections about this from the science-nerd community, who will try (in vain) to change my thinking by throwing things like *facts* at me – such as "The dwarf jellico is a *bush,* not a blob, and neither it nor any member of its immediate phylum has ever wreaked havoc while starring in a low-budget movie."

These science guys just *love* facts. And they hate guys who hate facts. Things could get messy. But don't worry about me – I can hold my own when it comes to intellectual rasslin' with science-nerds.

The thing for you, as a reader, to take away from all this is this: St. Helena offers a wonderfully wide variety of exotic species, and touring the island to see them is an absolutely unforgettable experience.

I really do suggest that you nature-lovers stay alert out there though. You actually may encounter The Giant Earwig. And if you do, put it in a mayonnaise jar and drop it off at your nearest Giant Earwigologist's.

He or she will be delighted.

Until the middle of the night, that is... when the beast suddenly bursts the jar into smithereens and starts galloping through a rapid-growth cycle until it's towering over the lab in a frenzied rage, dripping slime from its gaping jaws as it wildly flails its giant unmentionable bum-mounted pinchers...

Hey, maybe I aint no science-nerd, but I've studied a thing or two in my time.

MENACING BUM-MOUNTED PINCHERS

BUMMAL AREA

The Giant Earwig of St. Helena
– Labidura herculeana –
the world's largest earwig

Chapter Seventeen

Central Casting? Gimme a Guy with No Nose

The distant outposts of the world have always attracted adventurers. It's as if, like birds or salmon or reindeer, they answer some subconscious migratory call. This influx of adventurers, over a period of five hundred years, accounts for the disproportionately grand and rousing history of the tiny remote island of St. Helena.

At the end of this chapter I've included a list of historical dates. A glance at the list shows that some of history's heaviest hitters have played a part in the story of St. Helena: Charles Darwin. Captain Cook. Captain Bligh. Sir Edmund Halley (discoverer of Halley's Comet). Flab-fondler Napoleon Bonaparte. And the Napoleon-whuppin' Duke Of Wellington, to name but a few.

But their exploits are well documented and easily available to the reader. I recommend *St. Helena 1502-1938* by Philip Gosse – (see bibliography). So here I'll focus on a few of the lesser-knowns, whose stories lie hidden in the dusty pages of obscure St. Helenian history.

Submitted for your perusal: the weird events surrounding the unrenowned Mrs. J. H. Beck. Her strange, morbid, implausible and outlandish tale could easily have dripped from the pen of the imaginative

Stephen King. But her story comes to us from real life.

We learn of Mrs. Beck from the written reminiscences of one George Brooks Bennett. Mr. Bennett and Mrs. Beck were fellow passengers on *The Struan,* sailing from St. Helena to Cape Town in May, 1851. He describes Mrs. Beck as "a dear old lady" and then tells us how she came to be on her way home to Cape Town from St. Helena. (It is my italics that appear throughout the account.) She was

"the widow of the Reverend J. H. Beck, the pastor of the Mission Chapel in Long Street (Cape Town). His health failing him, he had been induced... to try a change of climate and proceed to St. Helena. He followed this advice but died on the voyage. Before he died, he begged of his wife, and of the Captain too, that he might be buried in the Country Churchyard at St. Helena... *This was promised.* When he died, a coffin was made by the carpenter of the ship, and covered with pitch and tar, and slung over the stern.

But unfortunately a dead calm followed, and the ship lay motionless for several days. The decomposing body became so offensive that at last it had to be cut adrift, and disappeared in the sea. Strange to say – within an hour after, they had a rattling breeze which carried them into St. Helena (after three days sailing).

The poor widow was inconsolable and yet she was so impressed with the idea that her husband's earnest wish to be buried in the Country Churchyard at St. Helena would be granted (*she and he too had prayed for this*) that she went down to the beach morning after morning in quest, and offered money to the boatmen to look for the coffin.

Incredible as it may appear, she did not leave St. Helena with the wish ungranted. A fisherman reported one day in town that he had seen a strange looking chest lying high and dry among the rocks to windward. *He said it was so strangely lodged among the rocks that the hand of God alone could have put it there.*

... A party of men was sent overland, and the strange looking chest was safely, but with great difficulty, hauled up. A glance at the box enabled Captain Carew to recognize the coffin constructed on board. It was duly opened and its occupant identified.

The widow's prayer had been answered, and she had the melancholy satisfaction of seeing her aged partner laid (in the Country Churchyard). ...This having been accomplished, she took her passage... with us in The Struan.

When one reflects that the vessel was about three days' sail from St. Helena at the time the body was committed to the deep, it is one of the most marvellous things on record that the coffin should have been wafted by the waves to such a speck as St. Helena..."

And to this day, The Reverend Beck's seafarin' coffin and remains rest in peace at the Country Churchyard. I located his grave after a diligent search through a vegetation-choked, neglected area of the sloping graveyard. The people buried there all died long ago and they and their graves have long since been forgotten. James Henry Beck's untended grave is overgrown with crotch-high grass and weeds. Two wild shrubs obscure the moss-flecked headstone. I parted the shrubs so I could read the strange epitaph inscribed on the tombstone:

In memory of The Rev. J.H. Beck who died on board the brig Jane, March 11th 1851 whilst on a voyage for his health. His remains most unexpectedly drifted and were washed on shore at St. Helena... Precious in the sight of the Lord, The death of His Saints...

Look again at a map and compare the size of the ocean to the size of St. Helena. *Was* it a Heaven-sent answer to a prayer? Ocean currents? ...or a prevailing wind from... *The Twilight Zone.*

dunno.

But while we're on the strange and morbid, I should mention my surprise at finding the name of Frederick Marryat in the cobwebbed annals of St. Helena's past. I had known of him since childhood, when I first read his excellent story *The Little Savage* (which I've re-read hundreds of times since). But besides being a widely read author, it seems Frederick Marryat was also a sailor, an artist, and a soldier in the British Regiment guarding Napoleon on St. Helena. Toward the end of his tour of duty on the island, at the request of the Governor, he did a drawing of the Emperor, who posed for him in bed – dead.

All this will come in handy if you're ever on a quiz show faced with tough questions from the "Strange And Morbid History Of Outposts" category.

But so much of the history of St. Helena seems as if it came straight out of some "Boys' Big Book Of Adventure" that I can't stop myself from describing the island's discovery in pirate-speak...

...Aye, Billy. 'Twas in 1502, and a Portuguese crew, dead-weary from sailin' the long voyage back to Portugal from India, was crossin' the South Atlantic — an ocean so vast and empty that a man starts thinkin' that all dry land everywhere has sunk to the bottom o' the sea!

And one day, Billy, they spies an island! All by itself. Mysterious lookin'. Risin' waaay up out o' the sea and shrouded in mist. No tellin' what such a place might be harbourin' — bloodthirsty savages and creatures and monsters as yet unknown! But bein' brave men, they musters up a landin' party and goes explorin'. Plunder a-plenty — fresh water, sea birds, seals an' turtles.

And not a soul around.

They was the first 'uns to set foot there since the dawn o' time itself. So they claims 'er in the name o' the King o' Portugal and christens 'er "Santa Helena".

But the Portuguese wasn't just brave sailors, Billy. They was also uncommon smart. They keeps quiet about that island ... for eighty-six years! So 'twas only Portuguese sailors as comes ashore to drink the fresh water and eat the fruit and recover from the scurvy that plagued all who dared to sail the vast landless South Atlantic.

Now p'raps yer wonderin' who might be the first man ever to live on that secret island. 'Twas Fernando Lopez. And his tale, Billy, is stranger than any you'll find in storybooks. ... Aye, 'tis much stranger indeed.

Hi, it's just me – I'm back. Sorry about that. Lapsing into pirate-speak is an occupational hazard when writing about those bygone days of sail.

When Cynthia and I learned of the life story of Fernando Lopez, we wondered why we hadn't heard it before. It seemed like something everyone should already know about – a great true story from the pages of history, full of tragedy and suffering and joy and triumph and larger-than-life but true events.

Cynthia and I were very moved by Fernando's little-known story and we thought others would be too. We considered writing a book about him, but when we thought about the backdrop to Fernando's story – the breathtaking scenery of St. Helena – we felt that no written description could properly tell the tale.

We decided that the best way to tell Fernando's story would be by shot-on-location technicolour movie. And we spent a year of our lives writing, re-writing and typing a screenplay about the life of Fernando Lopez.

We'd seen our fair share of movies, but neither of us had ever written a screenplay. So we both read several books on the subject, and then we began.

Screenplays are weird things. They are a specialized form of storytelling, organized on the page in a very specific way, with rules regarding the typed spacing and a particular kind of abbreviated, shorthand style of writing. The unique format of screenplays was devised so that each page of storytelling corresponds to one minute of screen-time. A 120-page screenplay describes a two-hour movie.

I will now attempt a synopsis of Fernando's life story, but as anyone who's ever read a TV guide knows, a synopsis can never articulate a story properly. It's the details, the nuances, the scenes and the scenery, the atmosphere and the little moments that make a story, or a movie, special. However, here are the (compressed) true facts of Fernando's story.

Fernando Lopez was a Portuguese officer and a gentleman stationed at Goa, India, in 1512. When the Indians of Goa rose up against the colonizing Portuguese, Fernando and several other Portuguese soldiers felt that the Indian's cause was just. So they joined the Indians and fought against their own countrymen. Eventually the Indians were forced to surrender, but they did so only on the condition that the Portuguese army spare the lives of Fernando and his fellow renegades. The cruel, devious Portuguese Commander did spare their lives... but he ordered that they be "punished" ...by mutilation. Each man had his right hand, his left thumb, his ears and his nose hacked off...and more than half the victims died from the mutilation. Fernando survived, only to go on to a very grim existence in India, shunned and despised.

In 1513, he stowed away on a ship bound for Portugal, hoping to return to his family. While at sea, he was discovered and put to work on the ship. As the long voyage dragged on, Fernando began to regret his decision to return to Portugal. He feared the burden of shame that his family would have to bear on his return.

So when the ship stopped to take on fresh water at the uninhabited island of Santa Helena, Fernando made a dash for the deep woods, and eluded the search parties.

Finally they sailed away, leaving him a barrel of biscuit, some dried fish, some beef, some salt, some old clothes and a fire.

Fernando dug himself a cave – with only one hand, minus the thumb, and no tools. He explored the beautiful island and found many edible plants. He also managed to catch fish.

After a year of solitude, a ship arrived. Fernando hid and eventually the ship sailed, leaving behind cheese, biscuits and rice for him. As he watched the ship sail off, a small bird was thrown from it into the sea. The pathetic sight of the struggling bird as it bobbed helplessly in the waves compelled Fernando to dive into the ocean and rescue it before it drowned. He carried the dripping bird to his cave, dried it by the fire and fed it some rice. It was a baby rooster – a cockerel. They became the best of friends. The little bird soon came when called and followed Fernando everywhere. At night they snuggled together in the bed in the cozy little cave, and Fernando experienced love in his life again.

Ten years passed happily, with Fernando and the bird hiding whenever a ship arrived, and collecting gifts that the sailors would leave. Among the Portuguese, Fernando was becoming a legend – a man living all alone on a remote island, the very existence of which was being kept secret from the rest of the world. He became known as "The Loneliest Man In The World." Eventually the King of Portugal heard of Fernando's plight and was very moved. He sent him a letter, urging him to return to Portugal and offering him safe passage.

While Fernando was mulling this over, a ship arrived. Among the landing party was a Javanese slave-boy, who ran for the woods, just as Fernando had, years before. The ship sailed without the lad, and Fernando was forced to share his island kingdom with him. Unlike the fictional Robinson Crusoe and Friday, the real-life Fernando and the boy from Java did not get along.

When the next ship arrived, the boy gave himself up and showed the ship's Captain where Fernando was hiding. The kindly Captain befriended Fernando and assured him that the King had declared that no one should remove Fernando from Santa Helena unless he wanted to leave.

Protected by the King's decree, Fernando began to show himself to sailors of the passing ships and to converse with them. Eventually he agreed to leave Santa Helena, bound for Portugal.

In Lisbon, Fernando met the King and Queen. They arranged an audience with the Pope in Rome, where Fernando confessed his sins and was given absolution. The Pope then asked him what he most wanted in life.

Fernando's only wish was to return to Santa Helena.

So his passage was arranged and he returned to his beloved island, to grow his garden and to tend a menagerie of animals. He continued to meet with the people of passing ships, but lived in happy solitude. He died in 1545, after nearly thirty years on Santa Helena.

This is an outline of the historic facts from which Cynthia and I created our screenplay. We immersed ourselves in the unfamiliar literary format because we wanted to tell Fernando's story in the medium most likely to do it justice. I saw Fernando's story as a cross between *Robinson Crusoe* and *The Elephant Man*. I envisioned sweeping panoramas of the island's natural beauty providing a dramatic setting for the poignant, true story of a cruelly abused giant of the human spirit. A man who escapes from the hell made by men and into a Garden Of Eden, where he develops a truly meaningful, loving relationship with a bird. Healed by the loving bond with the bird, he is eventually able to forgive human beings and to accept them back into his life.

Cynthia and I worked hard on the screenplay. But when it was finished we never showed it to anyone. We feared that it would be hacked to death by Hollywood.

I began to have a recurring nightmare in which a self-appointed-king-of-cool Hollywood producer is speaking to me with great enthusiasm: "I tellya Rex, it wasn't easy to cast – romantic leading man with no nose. But I signed the right guy! I smell money."

For Fernando

I wanted the world to honour your name.
I stupidly thought it meant Hollywood fame,
Brave, brave Fernando.

But Job Number One is to dumb the thing down
'cuz stupid sells big in Ol' Tinseltown,
Brave, brave Fernando.

They'd have you moon-walkin'
and callin' folks "dude"
and grabbin' your crotch
and dancin' real rude
and kick-boxin' bad guys with Bubbles The Chimp
and talk in a high girlie-voice like a wimp
and eyeballin' slave-boys with undisguised lust...

I think that the screenplay should just gather dust,
Brave, brave Fernando.

Historical Dates

1502 St. Helena was discovered by Admiral Juan da Nova Castella on 21st May. He built a chapel on the present site of St. James' Church using the timbers of an unseaworthy ship. The Portuguese left goats and used the island as a secret watering and victualling base.

1513 Dom Fernando Lopez became the first inhabitant.

1588 Captain Thomas Cavendish called at St. Helena on the homeward leg of his round the world voyage in *Desire*. The secret location of the island had been revealed to him by the captured pilot of a Spanish vessel that Cavendish had sunk in the Pacific. Thereafter the English and Dutch came frequently for fresh water and fruits, which grew in abundance on the island.

1605 – 1625 Portuguese/Dutch sea-battles left several wrecks in James Bay.

1633 The Dutch took possession of the island but abandoned it in 1651 when they settled in the Cape of Good Hope.

1659 Captain John Dutton was appointed as the first Governor of St. Helena under the English East India Company, who built the first permanent settlement at James Valley.

1660 – 1792 Slaves were imported, mostly from the East Indies and Madagascar.

1667 Refugee settlers from the Great Fire of London arrived.

1673 The island was captured by the Dutch on 1st January and retaken by Sir Richard Munden a few months later. New policies were instituted for conducting island affairs under a new charter granted by Charles II.

1676 Edmund Halley arrived on the island to observe the transit of Mercury and Venus.

1691 William Dampier, pirate, explorer and naturalist visited the island.

1723 The population of the island was 1,128, half of whom were slaves.

1733 *Coffee Arabica* from Mocha was planted. (Awarded First Prize at The London 1851 Exhibition.)

1760 The Royal Society sent Dr. Nevil Maskelyne to observe the transit of Venus.

1775 Captain Cook visited the island on his second circumnavigation of the world.

1784 St. James' Church was built. (Now the oldest Anglican church in the Southern Hemisphere.)

1792 Captain Bligh (of *Bounty* fame) arrived at the island with a cargo of breadfruit trees.

1792 The importation of slaves ended.

1805 Sir Arthur Wellesley, later Duke of Wellington, stayed on the island on passage home from India.

1810 The first Chinese indentured labourers arrived on the island.

1815 Napoleon arrived on St. Helena. He was forced to live in exile on the island after being defeated by the Duke of Wellington at the Battle of Waterloo.

1821 Napoleon died on St. Helena on the 5th of May.

1832 The East India Company finally abolished slavery on the island.

1834 The administration of St. Helena was transferred to the British Government after 162 years under the East India Company.

1836 Charles Darwin visited the island aboard the *Beagle*.

1840 Napoleon's body was exhumed and returned to France aboard the frigate *La Belle Poule*.

1840 – 1864 A Vice-Admiralty Court, a Royal Naval Squadron and an African Liberated Slave Depot were established on St. Helena to suppress the transatlantic slave trade. Hundreds of slave ships were captured and more than 10,000 Africans were liberated. White ants (termites) were imported in the timbers of a Brazilian slave ship.

1840 – 1914 The island served as a recruiting, refitting and trading base for American whaling fleets.

1844 – 1847 St. Helena served as a base for the West African coast guano trade.

1846 Thirteen ships were destroyed in James Bay by Atlantic rollers (large waves).

1869 St. Helena's importance as a port of call was greatly diminished with the development of steamships and the opening of the Suez Canal.

1890 Chief Dinizulu, leader of the African Zulus, began a seven-year internment on St. Helena, imposed by the British Government.

1898 Joshua Slocum, the first man to sail single-handed round the globe, visited St. Helena.

1899 The Eastern Telegraph Company laid the first link of submarine cable that connected St. Helena and Cape Town.

1900 General Cronje and 514 other Boer prisoners were sent to St. Helena.

1902 The last batch of Boer prisoners arrived, making a total of 6,000.

1903 All Boer prisoners departed.

1904 A ship, the *Papanui,* caught fire and sank in James Bay. The remains of the steering gear can still be seen above water.

1906 The British Army garrison withdrew. This caused much unemployment and financial hardship on the island.

1907 The successful introduction of the manufacture of fibre from New Zealand flax rescued the island from hardship and became the main source of income for the next sixty years.

1914 – 1918 The island was once again garrisoned.

1922 The island of Ascension, administered by the Admiralty, became a dependency of St. Helena.

1929 The first motor car, an Austin Seven, was brought to the island.

1941 The RFA *Darkdale* was sunk in the harbour by a German U-boat. Forty-one of the crew of fifty perished.

1947 King George VI, Queen Elizabeth, Princess Elizabeth and Princess Margaret visited the island.

1966 The flax industry collapsed. There was no longer a market for exported flax fibre because of the development of synthetic fibres.

1967 The Summer of Luvvy

1968 The first general election was held.

1973 Coins were minted to mark the tercentenary of the Royal Charter granted by King Charles II.

1982 The Falklands War re-affirmed the strategic importance of Ascension and St. Helena. The RMS *St. Helena* (a former Canadian Coast Guard vessel) saw service in the Falklands conflict.

1984 HRH Prince Andrew visited the island to commemorate the 150th anniversary of St. Helena becoming a Crown Colony.

1991 The new RMS *St. Helena*, purpose-built to service the island, made its maiden voyage.

2002 Princess Anne visited the island for a three day stay to commemorate the 500th anniversary of the discovery of the island.

2003 The Island's decreasing population hit a low of approximately 4,000 persons, the lowest since 1946.

2004 Rex Gandhi-Of-The-South-Atlantic declared his historic busting of Napoleon's curse.

Chapter Eighteen

Life is a Carnival:
Ya Pays Yer Money and Ya Takes Yer Chance!

The Saints, taken as a group, are not what you'd call "pushy." They are remarkably, and enjoyably, the very opposite. In general, there is a nonassertive, we-take-what-we're-given attitude, which struck me as being something belonging to an earlier period of history. Probably this passivity originated during the island's dark days of slavery, and continued through the subservient colonial period, eventually becoming a national habit, a philosophy, and a way of life. "Us not worry *that*, luvvy."

It's likely that St. Helena's exceptional isolation has also played a significant part in preserving and perpetuating this time-warped fatalism. Consumers here have always been faced with a take-it-or-leave-it situation. In the island's shops, prices are high, quality is often low and selection is very limited. And weird. For example, the "big" hardware store in Jamestown does not stock a bicycle tire pressure gauge, but *does* sell two different styles of coffin handles.

While riding along on my under- and over-inflated bike tires, I've been thinking about those coffin handles. And I'm thinking maybe they've got something there. I'm picturing D.I.Y. Prefab Coffin Kits.

187

- **Assembles easily in just two hours!** – no special tools required
- **Tough particle-board construction!** – peel-n-stick vinyl veneer looks just like hand-polished mahogany!**
  Come see the huge selection at Coffins-R-Us!

I'm hoping someone will take this idea, get rich, and in gratitude send me a bicycle tire pressure gauge. I realize that this roundabout way of getting a pressure gauge may be slow, but here on St. Helena, you learn to wait for things.

Since the island manufactures almost nothing and every "thing" must be imported, any item – used, scratched, dented, stained, obsolete or past the sell-by date – has acquired some value by the time it reaches St. Helena. There's always someone here who'll pay cash – on an "as is, where is, no guarantee given or implied" basis – for an item that would be consigned to the dumpster in The Big World.

And with the exception of gasoline and diesel fuel (which comes by tanker) everything arrives on the one and only ship. The monopoly on shipping pretty much strangles healthy capitalist competition, since each store pays the same high rate to import goods. The only way for merchants to sell products at anything like affordable prices is for them to import inexpensive products. So there's no such thing as a "discount store" on St. Helena. Instead, there's flimsy, tacky, knock-off, bargain-basement-type junk for sale at very high prices in every store.

Yet it's very rare to see someone returning shoddy goods.

Cynthia and I have done so, on occasion. The mortified store clerk will seek out the store owner and attempt to explain the inexplicable.

"What they want, see, they want to bring back this underarm deodorant! They say it don't work – won't come out-like."

The clerk and the owner look at us as if we just have to be a hallucination. Other shoppers stop and marvel, horrified, as if at a gruesome car accident. We explain that upon taking the deodorant home and opening it up, no deodorant bar would rise up from the container when we turned the dial on the bottom. So we would like to exchange it. For one that... works.

After much humming and hawing and inspecting, and re-inspecting and re-re-inspecting, and re-re-re-inspecting, the store owner very grudgingly exchanges it... but with a distinctly grim atmosphere of "Don't let it happen again" and an unsaid, "I'm letting you guys get away with this just this once, only because you're foreigners and you don't know any better, but just watch your step in future."

The bystanders marvel at our weird and wacky foreigner ways.

I'm willing to bet that no Saint has ever heard of crusading consumer watchdog Ralph Nader.

But perhaps the definitive demonstration of the "take-what-you're-given" mentality is the story of "Darrell." We met Darrell at the side of the road, while on his lunch break. He was working on repairing a stone wall. Like most Saints, Darrell is friendly and likeable. We passed by him often and always stopped to chat for a few minutes. We all enjoyed talking about the differences between Canada and St. Helena. One day I commented on the fact that so many Saints have tattoos. Darrell proudly showed us his, on his arm.

"I got that on Ascension Island," he said. "That not done at home with one pin and pen ink. That by one real tattoo artist with the real machine and made-for-the-purpose needles. It's true hey! It come from The Big World. That man come Ascension on one ship and all Saints what work on Ascension got one, see? So I got one too. I pay my money – I not like needles so I close my eyes and I hold out my arm like that," (he demonstrated: one arm stretched out straight; the other hand covering his eyes) "and I say that man 'Give me one please, Sir!'"

Darrell laughed happily at the memory of it.

"Do you mean you didn't choose the design?" I asked, somewhat incredulous. (After all, a tattoo is attached to your skin for your whole life.)

"No, I not do *that*! I not say that man 'give me *this* one' or 'give me *that* one'. I just say him 'give me one please,

Sir!' and he start up that machine – just for me! And I *got* one!" he said.

A proud and brave, satisfied customer.

Much later we learned that Darrell is gay. I tried to coordinate that information with the tattoo on his forearm. The tattoo of a naked woman.

Chapter Nineteen

Us Not Worry *That*, Luvvy

I looked fondly at the three big cardboard boxes sitting on the kitchen floor. They were somewhat crumpled from their long voyage through the postal system and half-way around the globe. And yet, because of the careful, clever packing job, nothing inside was broken. Cynthia's Mum had packed these boxes – full of practical, handy, impossible-to-get-on-St. Helena *stuff*. She had spent a whole year scanning catalogues, looking on the internet and rummaging through Goodwill shops for hard-to-find but perfect gadgets to help us in our off-the-map lifestyle.

She'd mailed these boxes in September and now our Christmas presents had arrived. Woo Hoo! Christmas! It was May.

I was touched by all the love and the care and the smarts that had gone into the shopping and packing. But I wasn't surprised. Cynthia's Mum is a kind, caring, clever and resourceful person.

She's also a bit of a worrier. In fact, she's what you might call a "gifted" worrier.

Wait. I'm wildly understating this.

A little more upfront: Cynthia's Mum is a shoo-in for

The Gold in the Mother's Freestyle at the World Worrying Olympics.

Hold on. I'm still pussyfooting.

Closer to the truth: if the aliens ever release a substance into Earth's atmosphere that completely melts the worry center in the brain of every breathing organism on this planet, only Cynthia's Mum will find a way. She'll probably train another organ to worry. A kidney perhaps.

So, yes, without putting too fine a point on it, she's a bit of a worrier, if you get my drift.

But lovely with it.

The boxes made me reflect on how much she'd gotten on board and supported her only daughter's decision to move to a foreign distant remote island. It was very good of her, especially when you consider that initially she hadn't been too thrilled with the idea.

When we first told Cynthia's Mum that we prairie landlubbers were going to ride on a *ship*, way out into the middle of the South Atlantic Ocean… to get to an isolated island, *WHERE EMERGENCY AIRLIFT EVAC IS IMPOSSIBLE BECAUSE PLANES CANNOT LAND THERE* ...and that we were planning to spend six months being foreigners among a tightly-knit isolated nation of five thousand people ...of whom we knew exactly *no-one*... we expected her to worry. But she surprised us. "Call me when you get there," was pretty much all she had to say.

We had withheld the fact that we were actually scouting out St. Helena as a potential permanent home. After all, we reasoned, St. Helena may not suit us, and then she would have worried about *that* needlessly. So we just told her we were going on a holiday. And we set off.

That's when Cynthia's Mum's worry center started telegraphing Urgent Red Alert Messages (URAMs) to the Frightening-Thought Receptors of her motherly brain.

Urgent Red Alert Messages emanating from the worry center of the human brain are not conscious, well-thought-out conclusions. They are the subconscious blurted irrational ravings that our brains produce from the mangled memorized snippets of bad late movies that we've ingested while dozing on the couch. All URAMs from a brain's worry center begin with *what if*.

So Cynthia's Mum's URAMs began, of course, with *what if* and then went on about shipwrecks and shark attacks, and cannibals with recipes that call for free-range Canadians, and tropical jungle-rot black-swamp galloping hoof-and-mouth voodoo-fortified delirium-fever.

But on a *conscious* level, Cynthia's Mum knew only that she was worried. So in an effort to ease her worrying mind, Cynthia's Mum tried to find out a bit about St. Helena. But back then, there was very little in print about the island, and no websites at all. Worse yet, no one she spoke to had ever even *heard* of the place.

Cynthia's Mum is not a sit-in-a-snit-type of worrier. She's a take-action-type worrier of the first order. So she phoned the operator in St. Helena and told the operator that she needed to talk to somebody on St. Helena to find out just exactly what kind of place they're running down there, because her only daughter was on the way there right now, on a *ship,* and of course, *anything could happen.*

The operator kindly explained that discussing multiple scenarios of projected doom and disaster with distraught mothers was not in her job description. She could only give out phone numbers. "Perhaps you'd like to speak to someone from The Chamber of Commerce?" offered the helpful operator.

"Yes. Let me speak to The Chamber of Commerce. That would be fine," said Cynthia's Mum.

Now that was a wise move. Because if anyone's going to keep accurate up to date statistics on the fiscal impact of voodoo-induced shark attacks and such, it's going to be The Chamber of Commerce.

A helpful member of The St. Helena Chamber of Commerce came on the line and I think it went sort of like this.

Cynthia's Mum: "Hello? I'm calling from Canada and here's the thing: My daughter's gone completely crazy! Somehow she got it into her head that she wanted to go to some god-awful jungle-island way the heck out in the absolute middle of nowhere, that nobody's even *heard* of, where who-knows-*what* goes on – maybe voodoo-related tropical jungle-rot black-swamp galloping hoof-and-mouth delirium-fever *or something*, and I'm worried sick!"

The Chamber of Commerce chap asked where we'd be staying on St. Helena, and Cynthia's Mum told him: Cambrian House in Jamestown. By coincidence, the Chamber of Commerce chap, Nick by name, owned Cambrian House and was to be our landlord. He explained this to Cynthia's Mum.

Cynthia's Mum: "Okay. What I want is the truth. Is there *any* hope she'll survive?"

Nick: "You really mustn't worry. Your daughter certainly won't have to contend with anything *like* what your thinking. But I'm afraid she *will* have to face something quite..."

Cynthia's Mum: *"What? Quite what?"*

Nick: "Well, it's just a bit... I should have *warned* her I suppose. Rather irresponsible of me really..."

Cynthia's Mum: "WHAT? *TELL* ME! *WHAT?*"

Nick: "Well... I'm afraid she may have to fend off rather a lot of invitations to tea from the elderly lady that lives next door."

*　　　*　　　*

Blissfully oblivious to the lurking fate that awaited us, Cynthia and I arrived on St. Helena.

Within ten minutes, I knew I'd be happy to live on the island. Cynthia, always cautious, resisted the island's charms for nearly three days.

My first impression of Jamestown was that it was warm and sunny and pleasant and quaint and bustling and small. (How small is "small" you ask? Fact: years later I was standing on *the* street *in* Jamestown, when a tourist asked me if I knew where he could catch a bus *to* Jamestown.)

For me, Jamestown had just the right amount of peeling paint. Not too shabby and rundown, but authentic. Honest. And endearing. A breath of fresh air after The Big World's slick synthetic contrived environments. I knew right away – it's got soul. And good vibe. Smiling people call out to each other everywhere.

"Luvvy! You alright?"

"Not too bad!"

Vanessa, Nick's polite, conscientious property manager, drove us and our luggage up from the wharf to Cambrian House. We were speechless as she showed us around the place. Cambrian House is an elegant stately home tastefully furnished with beautiful antiques. On the large front veranda a big brass ship's bell serves as a doorbell. Inside, the large airy whitewashed rooms were all spotlessly clean and welcoming. We toured the extensive grounds, admiring the large vegetable garden, the mango trees full of mangos and chattering mynah birds, and a towering palm tree. I, a connoisseur of an art form I like to think of as "moveable metal sculpture,"(more commonly known as antique cars) bonded instantly with a rusting 1940s Austin touring car parked in the garage. The king and queen of England and their two princess daughters had toured the island in it during their historic visit to the island in 1947. Bright bougainvillea flowers splashed a vibrant crimson all over the scene. The house and grounds were, by anyone's standards, beautiful. Very classy, but relaxed. We loved it.

Then Vanessa introduced us to the elderly next-door neighbour.

*   *   *

Her name was Molly, and over the months we spent many happy hours with her, learning about the island, drinking tea, and trying to grasp her unique assessment of the local political scene.

"Oh he's very good. The radio interviews about his embezzlement charges were lovely – such a nice deep *manly* voice!"

Or she might say, "Her? She's smart, she's honest and she cares about the people. She could do a lot for this island, but she really mustn't wear that hideous blue sweater!"

And so on.

Molly kind of fascinated me. I'd never met anyone at all like her. She was in her eighties, a feisty old Empire Builder, carrying on in one of the few remaining overlooked and forgotten fragments of the vanished Empire. She'd left England as a young bride and spent almost her entire adult life in Rhodesia as the wife of a British mining engineer. In the early 1960s Molly and her husband were returning to England to retire, when the ship they were on called in briefly at St. Helena. Her husband fell in love with the island, and the ship left without them.

Sometimes Molly would fall into a melancholy mood. She'd tell me again about how her husband had chosen St. Helena for them as a home, and had then had the gall to up and die on her – abandoning her on this remote island, when she'd have been so much better off in England.

"And now I'm stuck here, all alone. Thousands of miles from England. Oh dear, oh dear..."

I'd try to cheer her up.

"It's not like that at all, Molly! You've got everything going for you here! You've got a nice flat in a beautiful old house in sunny Jamestown and lots of caring friends; and a nice librarian who pencils your initials into the library books you've read so your friends can select new library books for you. And the police come by and tap on your door every evening just to make sure you're alright and to have a little chat. And you live with your doors and windows wide open without fear of being victimized by heartless cowardly criminals who pray on the elderly. Believe me Molly, there are legions of elderly people in England – and all over the world! – who'd trade places with you in a heartbeat!"

Molly would brighten. "Really? Do you think so?"

"I *know* so!"

Then Molly would press me for details. "Is it *really* all that dreadful out there?"

So I'd cheer her up by telling her how awful The Big World had become. I'd tell her (in my deepest voice) of The System's ongoing indifference to The Big World's ongoing, shocking, predatory brutality... and about the gross corruption in high places... and about legally-sanctioned injustice. It was pretty heavy stuff. But *still* Molly didn't see St. Helena as a life raft of peace and pleasantness on the very troubled waters of Modern Times.

One day though, I really struck a nerve.

I spoke of the unspeakable.

I told her about a horror she'd never heard of: telemarketing.

"You see, Molly, complete strangers phone you up to sell you... carpet cleaning."

"I don't understand. If they don't know me how can they possibly know that my carpets want cleaning?"

"They don't. They just phone *everybody in the whole phonebook* and *ask* them if they want their carpets cleaned."

"Surely not!"

"*Oh* yes. So you *just* get into a nice hot bath, and the phone rings. And because it *may* be important, you *have* to get out and answer the phone. And when you get there, dripping wet, you find it's just someone you don't know trying to sell you carpet cleaning that you don't need."

"Oh no! Oh dear! ...Are you quite sure about this?"

"Yep. So you tell them no thank you and you go and get back into your tub, and the phone rings *again*."

"But you've already *told* them you don't want your carpets cleaned. I don't understand!"

"Yes, you've told *them* you don't want your carpets cleaned, but this is somebody *else*... wanting to know if you'll buy some *light bulbs* ...or some *magazines*... or some *dance lessons*... *or if you'd care to help a brand new religion purchase sequined jump-suits for its choir*." ("Hi, I'm calling on behalf of The New Church Of The Super-Double-Jesus-And-Extra-Holy-Saints and...")

"No!"

"Molly, it's not pretty, but it's a fact. Nowadays people in The Big World pay every month for the privilege of being continually harassed."

"Oh dear, oh dear, oh *dear!*"

Horrifying little old ladies isn't my usual line of work... but any job worth doing is worth doing right. And I really think Molly began to view her situation on St. Helena in a more positive light. It's amazing what a simple tweaking of The Frightening-Thought Receptors can do.

Chapter Twenty

Don't Call Me "Lazy" When I Re-tire

No one knows why, but The Saints are keen on nicknames. And apparently this has been going on for quite awhile...

While travelling on the ship, Cynthia and I happened upon an exceptionally friendly and pleasant Saint. He was a crew member, and he worked the all-night watch. We'd sit on deck in the evenings outside the wheel-house and chat with him. He was very knowledgeable about the twinkling dome above us, and pointed out all kinds of planets and constellations to us. He also told us some good sea-farin' tales and some funny life-on-St. Helena stories.

Those late nights on the deck were pleasant. They had a dream-like quality to them, maybe because the setting was so beautiful and other-worldly. We were waaay out on the South Atlantic, far from all land and all lights, far even from shipping lanes and airplane routes. Only our little ship gliding through endless ocean beneath endless stars, with a warm wind, in from Africa, blowing gently against us like a good song.

And being in such good company made the entire Kodak moment even better. When we got around to exchanging names, he told us he was "Loogoo." I commented that it was, for me, an unusual name, and asked what it meant. Loogoo didn't know. It was his nickname, he said. So I asked him how he got it, expecting a funny story about a silly childhood incident, perhaps involving the mispronunciation of something while learning to speak.

But Loogoo looked a little surprised that anyone would ever ask anyone how he or she came by his or her nickname. It's like asking someone, "Where'd you get your pancreas?"

He thought for a second and then told me, "It's my brother's nickname too."

"Really?" I probably looked a bit surprised myself.

"Yes. And my daddy's, too."

"Wow," says I.

"And *his* daddy too. Us *all* Loogoos!"

So again I asked him why. (I simply *must* know where you got that pancreas!)

"Dunno. My granddaddy got that name way back in The Before Days. Me an' my brother, us is both Loogoo, but one is *Black* Loogoo, and one is *White* Loogoo."

I found this a bit bewildering – briefly. Then suddenly I figured it out. St. Helena must be one of those islands where everyone is nicknamed a different colour Loogoo.

But it turns out that not everyone on St. Helena *is* nicknamed Loogoo after all. I realized that after meeting Small Change.

Small Change came over one day to cut a doorway through our cement kitchen wall with a petrol-powered cement saw. It was noisy, dirty, dusty work and eventually we stopped to wash down some dust with some coffee. We got talking and, of course, I couldn't resist asking Small Change where he got his nickname. And this he told me:

He'd been on Ascension Island (700 miles northwest of St. Helena) for many years, working for the Americans at their military base. He worked with a group of Saints in the motor pool. His job was changing tires, but to make a dull job in a sleepy outpost interesting and challenging, Small Change became a self-appointed one-man Grand Prix pit crew. As soon as a vehicle was parked in the motor pool garage, he became a blur, wasting not a single motion or moment. He was dubbed "Small Change" in recognition of his excellent lightning-fast work.

It's alternately terrifying and entertaining to imagine what The Saints might nickname you. What would *your* nickname be if *you* moved to one of those islands where everybody's nicknamed after their tire-changing skills? I know what they'd call me. But it's long and derogatory.

I'd prefer "His Excellency" as a nickname, but it seems that one's already taken – by the Governor of St. Helena (who must be an absolute whiz at changing tires). I guess I could settle for "Your Rexcellency." It's short, vaguely complimentary, and implies that some sort of respect is due. Lemme test-drive this.

"Hi, I'm Rex, but friends just call me 'Your Rexcellency.'"

Ooh yeah, I like it! So much more up-market than "Can Change A Tire If He Really Has To But Does A Whole Lotta Whining First."

Chapter Twenty-One

A Puzzle Wrapped in an Enigma
– Instead of Blood and Sex

I'm very proud of my blue leather wallet. It's well-made, and on the front, embossed in gold, is the insignia of the RMS *St. Helena*, a sea serpent holding a crown. Very classy. Much more "executive" than my other stuff. But my pride of ownership does not stem from the fact that it's an up-market posh thing; I'm proud to own it because I received the wallet as an *award*.

For a Professional Ne'er-Do-Well to receive an award is an immeasurably rare event. It is almost unheard of. We in the Profession tend not to have Annual Awards Dinners to recognize and honour Outstanding Individual Contributions To Never Doing Well. We are unfamiliar with the applause of our colleagues. In our homes you will find an almost glaring absence of trophies and framed certificates and engraved mementos of appreciation. Usually, year in and year out, generation after generation, our achievements go unnoticed and unsung.

And that's as it should be. We do not enter the Profession to gather awards. We do what we do solely because we are called to it. The Professional Ne'er-Do-Well answers a strange call that very few can hear.

Unfortunately, on the one and only occasion that

my work as a Professional-Ne'er-Do-Well *was* publicly honoured, I was not present to witness the phenomenon and to participate in it.

The year was 1996. Cynthia and I had just spent six months on the island, investigating its suitability as a future home for us. We had decided that it would be a good place to live. Our plan was to return to Canada, sell up, and go back to St. Helena to stay.

We had been at sea for many days, voyaging from St. Helena to Cardiff, when this unexpected event transpired. I had skipped the ship's Award's Ceremony because I had assumed, naturally, that it could in no way involve me. The next day I was astonished to be (unceremoniously) handed the expensive wallet.

Having been raised on the Canadian prairie, my constitution is especially unadapted to ocean travel, and I had to resort to the only remedy that I find effective – mass consumption of anti-nausea pills. I had no choice but to accept the side effects: severe stupidity and insomnia.

Fourteen twenty-four-hour days is a lot of time to kill. Reading was out of the question because I had trouble comprehending the meaning of individual words, let alone complete sentences. The ship offered a wide variety of organized diversions and competitions but I was much too stupid to join in complicated games like deck quoits, and much, much too stupid to join in dangerous games like clay pigeon shooting. Deciphering the fun of a fancy dress party was far beyond my reach, as was following the plot of any movie.

This last limitation turned out to be only a minor drawback. The crew chronically selected movies that were wildly inappropriate for the mainly elderly passenger demographic. One morning at breakfast I asked an elderly gent if he'd enjoyed the previous evening's movie. He replied that it was the same as every movie he'd seen on board. "Awful – all just blood and sex."

Fortunately though, there was one distraction provided which suited me. I found that my mental capabilities could *just* be stretched to penetrate the complexities of assembling a jigsaw puzzle, provided I worked at my own pace. By that I mean that most of the time I sat motionless, staring blankly at the puzzle. Very occasionally I'd attempt to place a piece.

The blank staring proved to be the perfect activity for me. My task harmonized nicely with the hypnotic drone of the ship's engines and the vacant white noise inside my head.

The puzzle was set on a card table outside the Purser's Office, in the main reception area of the ship. Being a high-traffic area, many people passed through, and occasionally someone would stop to chat and maybe put in a piece or two. But my social skills were dulled. I could sense it. For example, at the time, my idea of a witty conversational rejoinder was "...Um..." Soon most people just hurried past, leaving me to continue my chosen enterprise of vacuous staring at either the puzzle pieces or the picture on the box.

I was able to sleep only an hour or two at a time, and as an alternative to tossing and turning in my tossing and turning bunk, I'd get dressed and go back to staring at the puzzle. At first, the after-hours drinkers would express their surprise at seeing me staring at the puzzle at three a.m.

"Whazziss... you shhtill here?...?"

And the early-birds en route to watch the sun rise over the ocean were similarly startled.

"Good God, man! Do you mean to tell me you've been sat there all night?"

Since my usual clever retort was to shift my zombie stare from the puzzle to the questioner, they soon learned to leave me to it and go about their business without acknowledging my furniture-like presence.

Somehow time passed.

When the puzzle was first placed out on the table it was announced that there would be a prize if it could be completed by the time we reached Tenerife. Tenerife was many nautical miles behind us, and the puzzle was nowhere near being finished.

Tick-tock, tick-tock. Days. Hours. Nights. Mornings. Afternoons.

Almost imperceptibly, the puzzle progressed. As it drew closer to completion, interest from the passengers and crew revived. "Oh my!" they all said with genuine surprise. "You *have* been busy! I didn't think you had a ghost of a chance of finishing it before we reach Cardiff, but perhaps you just may!" Then they'd study it awhile and maybe try to get in a piece or two before moving on.

Finally there were only a handful of pieces left to put in. The picture was of an English garden. All the remaining pieces were of blue sky, but there was a hole in the green flower stalks.

After various people told me that a piece was missing, it occurred to me that a piece was missing.

Various people suggested that maybe someone had pocketed the piece so that they could be the one to finish the puzzle. This got me thinking: maybe someone had *pocketed* the piece! ...so that *they* could be the one to finish the puzzle!

That such a dastardly scheme could be afoot was abhorrent to me, but when I considered my shipmates it seemed altogether too likely. I was among a bizarre international assortment of oddballs on an off-the-beaten-track cruise from one of the most remote inhabited islands in the world... and there was a high probability that someone on board was just cracked enough to want to turn the cruise into an Agatha Christie *Murder-On-The-Orient-Express*-style whodunnit.

So somewhere in the North Atlantic, off the coast of Spain, the jigsaw puzzle ceased to be a simple jigsaw puzzle. It was now a puzzle wrapped in an enigma. What had begun as a mindless means of passing time was now a highly complex task of criminal detection, involving sophisticated psychological analysis of both character and motive, as well as careful sifting and dissection of all the known facts. A daunting task for a pill-sodden sailor who high-fived himself if he managed to tie his shoes.

Everyone became a suspect and I became the enigmatic detective, quietly confident and well-versed in my own strange methods. I became this because, as we all know, enigmatic detectives who are quietly confident and well-versed in their own strange methods always unnerve devious culprits, causing them to make a stupid and fateful mistake. Every look, every word, every avoidance was another potential clue.

My first act of ingenious sleuthing was to continue to sit and stare at the puzzle, while cleverly refraining from putting the last few pieces in place. By means of this slick dodge I provided myself with a valuable ally: time. For I knew that the evil mastermind behind all this would not step from the shadows and reveal his or herself until they were sure that they alone possessed what would be the last piece of the puzzle.

And so I found myself involuntarily locked in a nerve-racking battle of wits with a brilliant criminal intellect. But I took heart from my shrewd opening move. I had stymied the fiend by cunningly forcing a temporary stalemate.

I began to consider the suspects.

The first that came to mind was the wealthy middle-aged woman collecting countries. Of British descent, she had been born and raised in Japan. Ten years or so ago she had joined a club in California in which the members compete to "collect" countries. For a country to be considered "collected" the member must have spent a minimum of twenty-four hours there. As a result, this woman had been travelling for a decade, and had "collected" something like one hundred and forty-two countries, St. Helena being the most recent.

She had absolutely no interesting tales of travel to tell. If asked about her experiences in, say, Bolivia, she was liable to concede that she had flown into La Paz at night, taken a taxi to the nearest Hilton Hotel, spent the night there and the day beside the pool and flown out again in the evening – happy to scratch another item off the list in her warped scavenger hunt. She had a twisted sense of competition and evidently enjoyed "winning" at demented games – a very likely suspect.

But by no means the only one. The dapper and outgoing little British chap was an obvious liar, and therefore, possibly bent enough to have done the deed. He had tried to pass himself off as a retired dentist, but this fatuous fiction was overtly contradicted by his mouthful of rotten teeth and his shocking halitosis. He was extremely well-groomed in every other respect and he dressed expensively and impeccably. Although markedly gregarious, he took pleasure only from speaking. He spoke with authority and intelligence, and gleefully launched into tortuous minutae on a wide variety of subjects – ranging from the preservation of architectural details of early Byzantine Churches to the menu items on board German Zeppelins.

It was clear that he regarded listening to anybody as a tiresome chore, and from this I concluded that when at work, he had been paid to listen. It struck me, Watson, that he must be a holidaying psychiatrist, concealing the nature of his true occupation as a means of avoiding the agony of listening to people's sordid problems. I further conjectured that such a man would be unlikely to suffer any ethical or moral dilemma if he decided to pocket the puzzle piece in order to study my reaction. Perhaps he was planning to present a paper at an upcoming psychiatrist's convention: "The Effect Of Treachery On A Zombie Exhibiting Furniture Syndrome."

My next task was to consider the disgruntled Australian widow whose hostility increased constantly as we sailed on. She complained bitterly to anyone who would listen that the ship's officers were acting irresponsibly and shirking their duty.

Her charge was that they weren't paying enough attention to the unescorted mature lady passengers. Given any opportunity she would eagerly report the latest scandalous statistics – the shamefully inadequate number of times any officer had asked her to dance.

"After all," she spat, "that's what they're getting paid

for! This ship's all computerized – it runs itself! They don't need showy young men to stare at a computer. Their job is to flatter those of us in our golden years – *and they're bloody well not doing it!*"

Her acrimonious rant grew crankier with each nautical mile. By degrees, the focus of her scorn slowly broadened until it included the entire male population of the earth and sea. And although I was seen as furniture, I was male furniture, and therefore sabotage-worthy. She had motive, and belonged on my list of suspects.

Which grew longer the longer I stared at the scene of the crime and pondered. The low-life millionaires needed to be considered. They and their gleaming white Rolls-Royce had boarded at Tenerife, and their arrival was difficult to ignore. They had a habit of yelling to and at each other from distant parts of the ship. It is possible they were hard of hearing; it is definite they were both always fully sauced. They were the quintessential loud, crude, obnoxious, garish, chain-smoking drunks.

It was hard to believe they had not stepped off the set of a bad TV sit-com, but they were for real. They had won the UK football pools and become instant millionaires. Somewhere they had gotten the idea (probably from watching bad TV sit-coms) that as rich people, they were obligated to treat everyone like dirt. I sensed that somehow through the alcoholic fog they dwelled in, they knew they were being snickered at, but they shrugged it off with their favourite expression: "Bugger it!"

They looked bizarre – he with his ascot, silk shirts and navy blue blazer, attempting to look like the suave playboy captain of a luxury yacht, but appearing instead to be a boozy middle-aged plumber off to a costume party... and she, bloated, pissed and oblivious, and made all the more ugly by the heaps of flashy jewelry attached to her corpulent mass. She had long ago mastered the delicate art of loud yelling with a burning cigarette dangling from the lips, and she gave frequent exhibitions of her skill.

They both drank in the ship's lounge from when they awoke till when they nose-dived at night. In the lounge they took nonstop tag-team turns feeding coins into the slot machine, or "one-armed bandit" or, in the hilarious euphemistic vernacular of the wholesome prissy British, "the fruit machine."

The low-life millionaires had the crazy idea that they owned everyone and everything, and could do, say, or have anything they wanted, which would of course include a piece of a jigsaw puzzle if the notion took their drunken fancy. And so, with an involuntary mental shudder, I placed them on my growing list of likely suspects.

The clock was ticking and I was starting to sweat. So far, being enigmatic and quietly confident and well-versed in my own strange methods had failed to unnerve any culprit, causing them to make a stupid and fateful mistake. In less than three days the ship would dock in

Cardiff, and the "perp," as American cops say (short for "perpetrator"), would "do a runner," as British cops say (long for "run away").

"What to do?" I wondered. "What to do?"

I have no idea how long I sat there thinking, "...Um...," my thought blending beautifully with the ship's engines' endless "hmmmmmm," but suddenly, out of nowhere, a blinding perception seared my psyche: This was not a case for Sherlock or Columbo or Poirot! What was needed here was the thinking of *Andy Warhol*.

A quick rummage through our cabin provided the required apparatus and I immediately set about creating Art That Is Indistinguishable From Machine-Made Images. The sun was just rising over the sea as I stood up to assess my finished work. The piece could be differentiated only by viewing the puzzle from a very oblique angle. Careful observation from that perspective revealed that it was just a shade less glossy than the others. Otherwise it was perfect.

I put in the pieces of sky.

"Well congratulations, you've done it!" exclaimed the first early-bird with surprise. "Where did you find the missing piece?"

Her question caused me a slight pang of suspicion, but I let it go. I explained what I'd done but she refused to believe me, even when I pointed out the piece. Finally, I showed her the trick of the oblique viewing. She was delighted.

Throughout the day all the passengers played a little game in which those who knew the viewing trick challenged those who didn't to find the handmade piece. No one who didn't know the trick could pick it out. There was a happy party-game atmosphere and I was complimented generously on my artistic skill.

No criminal mastermind stepped from the shadows to confess and I got to wondering if I'd misjudged my shipmates.

Perhaps the piece had just fallen on the floor and was accidentally vacuumed up by the cleaning staff?

That evening, in the ship's Main Lounge, the Ship's Awards Ceremony was held, and in a ritual rarely performed on earth, the work of a Professional Ne'er-Do-Well was publicly honoured. The wallet was awarded to me (in absentia) for all the entertainment provided to the ship's company as they tried to guess which puzzle piece was made by hand.

Meanwhile, having no puzzle to occupy myself with, I attended some forgettable movie in the Sun Lounge. I couldn't follow the plot, possibly because there wasn't one. My only recollection of the movie is that it *was* awful. All just blood and sex.

Chapter Twenty-Two

With a Bent Safety-Pin Through the Lip

Deepwater Jack and The Bastard Five Finger. They're from St. Helena. And they're good. But you're not gonna catch 'em down at The Pukin' Skunk or *any* Big World punk palace. Ya gotta catch 'em in St. Helena.

In the sea. They're two of the ten species of fish found only in the waters around St. Helena Island. These endemic fish are interesting for a variety of reasons, but the thing that really fascinates me is this: Who gave them their common names? And what was he on at the time? For example, the guy names one fish "Deepwater Jack" and another fish "Deepwater *Gurnard*." I bet the teasing never stops when you're named Deepwater Gurnard. (*Please!* Just call me 'Deep'.)

But we haven't come to the strange names yet. How about "The St. Helena Dragonet"? Perhaps the correct spelling is Dragonette and the "fish" is actually a small underwater dragon.

"Skulpins"? What kind of name is that? Somehow faintly derogatory, if you ask me – suggestive of a furtive, loitering, dishonest fish. And how about "Bastard Cavelley Pilot?" Wha? *Bastard Cavelley Pilot?* Fine, if you happen to be a ruthless World War One flying ace named Cavelley – but for a *fish?*

Now try this quick multiple choice quiz:

If a fisherman were to approach you on St. Helena and say, "I caught Springer's Blenny," the correct response would be:
 a) "I am disinterested in your sex life."
 b) "That damn Springer oughta keep his Blenny indoors."
 c) " Lucky you! That endemic fish will make an exotic and tasty meal."
The correct answer is, of course: "c, and by the way, a."

But for those who can see beyond the strange names, St. Helena is a fisherman's paradise. The island offers deep-water sport fishing for bullseye and grouper, as well as a variety of tuna – bigeye, yellowfin, albacore, and skipjack. In the high season, April to August, there is also wahoo, sailfish and marlin. You can join the local fishermen on one of their boats and go out for the day, setting out at dawn. Bring your own equipment or hire it from the local fishermen. No nets are used. Most boats work one or two heavy-duty sportfishing rods with multiplier reels.

The trip to the offshore fishing grounds can take an hour or so, and the enjoyment of being out on the beautiful blue sea is enhanced by sighting schools of playful dolphins and the amazing flying fish.

The other way to fish the waters of St. Helena is to fish from shore – either from costal rocks, or from a wharf in Jamestown or Rupert's Bay.

Fishing from the rocks usually involves a long hike down to the coast, as there are few spots on the island where sea level can be reached by road. But the walks themselves are exhilarating and rewarding. The ancient trails were made by fishermen and their donkeys, and they zig-zag down steep rock faces through unforgettable scenery. Bullseye, soldiers and silver fish can be caught from the rocky shoreline using only a simple bamboo rod and nylon line. I strongly urge the hiring of a local guide, as both the paths and the ocean swells can be tricky. Local fishermen often camp overnight at their favourite coastal spot, and attract the rockfish with ingenious homemade candle lanterns made from a glass bottle.

Fishing from the wharf in either Jamestown or Rupert's is a great way to meet the friendly Saints, and an easy alternative for those who aren't up for the strenuous (but rewarding) hike to the foot-access-only coastal fishing spots.

The sea around the island is teeming with fish, the water is clear and clean, the weather is great, and the local fishermen are friendly and helpful. No sport fisherman will be disappointed by a fishing trip to St. Helena.

And if you do come for the fishing, try not to think of the strange names of the endemic fish as "strange." Think positive. Think of them as "catchy."

Chapter Twenty-Three

Neil and Winnie and Bobby and Nort:
A Ballad Just Waiting to Happen

The Saints don't have much experience with Big World celebrities. And that's probably a good thing. There's a general feeling on St. Helena that *everybody* is *somebody*. Local celebrities are shown a quiet respect, not God-status.

The celebrity-obsessed Big World could learn a thing or two from these down-to-earth Saints.

As a young man in Winnipeg, I was always coming across old guys who just couldn't wait to tell me every trivial detail about the time they sold a hot dog to The Prime Minister, or shined Sammy Davis' shoes or drove The Monkees' limousine... and I always thought, Gods, if I ever get like that, please kill me.

The Gods never listen to me.

I'm an old guy now.

*   *   *

I'm not sure if Neil Young remembers me. It was a long time ago. He was in The Squires, just another of the hundreds of teenage rock-and-roll bands that erupted like acne all over Winnipeg in the Beatle-booming early '60s.

The Squires were having band practice upstairs at Neil's Mum's house on Grosvenor Avenue and I was "collecting" for my paper route. It was a weekly paper called (prophetically, I now realize) *The Star Weekly*. I delivered each Saturday, and once a month, as I delivered, I'd collect the money for the paper. I could hear the band practicing upstairs:

> *"Put on yer red dress baby...*
> *because we're goin' out tonight!*
> *Put on yer red dress baby...*
> *because we're goin' out tonight!*
> *Put on yer high heel sneak-ers...*
> *in case some foo-ool wants a fight!"*

I have loved rock-and-roll ever since the first five seconds of the Beatles' first appearance on *The Ed Sullivan Show*.

I rang the doorbell but they couldn't hear it. So I crouched beside the side-door doorstep and listened and grooved and waited. It was way too cold to sit on the frozen cement.

> *"For-your-love*
> *I'd give the moo-oon*
> *and the stars high above."*

Between tunes I'd lean on the doorbell and knock on the door, hoping to be heard amidst the guitar-tuning, drum-thrashing and musical noodling. Eventually someone caught on and Neil came downstairs to the door.

"Hi. Collecting for *The Star Weekly*," says I. I handed him the newspaper.

"Uh... how much is it?" says Neil. I told him – sixty cents.

"Oh. Just a minute, come in," says Neil.

I stepped inside and closed the door against the icy air. We were standing on a small landing, with one set of stairs going up into the house and another set going down into the basement. He called up the stairs to ask if anybody could lend him sixty cents. The response was a chorus of "No."

Neil looked at me and shrugged, helllp-less, helpless, he-elpless.

"Can you come back later? My Mum's out and I don't have any money."

My face sagged. The ball-and-chain around every newspaperboy's leg: people who didn't have the money on collecting days. It screwed the whole thing up. It meant a long freezing walk, covering the whole route twice and sometimes three times. A serious ordeal when it's forty below zero. It's the kinda thing that makes a guy wish his paper route was on a tropical island.

I stared dejectedly at my receipt book. The music had me feeling so good, and this was such a bring-down. A brief silence hung between us during which Neil shifted uneasily. He accidentally bumped a six-pack of empty pop bottles and they clinked.

"Hey!" he said, "If you want I could pay you in pop

bottles. There's more down in the basement, probably about two bucks worth. You can have 'em all. You can cash 'em at Bell's Drugstore over on Corydon."

I calculated swiftly: three blocks to Bell's... two bucks ...big cash. "Yeah sure!"

So Neil Young and I carried up all the pop bottles from his basement and put them outside on the step. I surveyed the pickins. Looked like over two bucks worth. Mostly big five-centers. Hardly any two-centers. I was rich.

"Okay then?" Neil asked.

"Yeah, *really* okay. Thanks!"

Neil went in and closed the door. While I was loading wealth onto my aluminum toboggan the music started up again:

"Gee-ell-oh-are-eye-A!
GLOW-OH-OH-REE-AHHH!"

I crouched beside the toboggan and listened. The band was good. But the cold was seeping into me and soon I had to move on, towing the toboggan carefully around snow-lumps to prevent bottle-loss. I think it was 1963... around forty years ago.

Like I say, I'm not sure if he remembers me.

He might though. I was the guy with the aluminum toboggan. The aluminum toboggan with the yellow rope. Not every newspaperboy had an executive-style aluminum toboggan back then. So Neil Young may or may not remember me, I don't know.

*   *   *

And I'm not sure if Winnipeg remembers Neil Young. His house remains unmarked and unknown. Almost anywhere else in the world it would be a must-see museum filled with rare and interesting memorabilia. But in Winnipeg? Not even a plaque.

Perhaps this is because Winnipeg is trying to make itself famous as The Winnie-The-Pooh Capital Of The World, although the connection between Winnie and Winnipeg is disputed by many. Some claim that A.A.Milne got the inspiration for the name "Winnie" from his time spent in Winnipeg. They allege that Mr. Milne encountered the muzzled black bear that was chained up each day outside a Portage Avenue bar to attract customers.

Bar patrons would get the bear very drunk and then wrestle it, "for entertainment." Some proud Winnipegers assert that "Winnie – The Bear Of Very Little Brain" was named after the drunken degraded miserable animal that low-life piss-artists enjoyed abusing on Winnipeg's main street.

Seizing on this obvious source of civic pride, the City Fathers have organized The Annual Winnie-The-Pooh Picnic In The Park. They intend to put Winnipeg on the map and attract world-wide tourism with this.

Understandably, that's a big job.

So it's easy to see how the city could overlook a self-taught musical genius who has penned countless timeless classics and brought pleasure to an international audience of millions in a phenomenal career spanning five decades. I guess the thinking down at City Hall is: Neil…? Neil? *Big fat schmeal!* Local drunks never beat *him* up for laughs, and there's no famous teddy-bear named "Neilie."

But Winnipeg is not alone in this snubbing of the local boy who makes good. It must be a mid-Western thing. Take, for example, the true facts of a tale that I shall call "Nort Steski And The Silver Strings."

NORT STESKI AND THE SILVER STRINGS

by Rex Bartlett

Once upon a time, around 1975, Nort Steski and I got into his VW bug and drove south, heading for Hibbing, Minnesota, USA — Bob Dylan's hometown.

Nort and I had played in a band together years before and were thinking of starting another band. I played keyboards and Nort played guitar. One day, in a Joan-Of-Arc kind of mood, I prophesized that if we bought silver guitar strings from the music shop in Hibbing where Bob Dylan had bought his first guitar, such strings would be magic strings, and our musical enterprise would be guaranteed of success. Nort concurred with this supernatural logic and we motored south from Winnipeg.

We were in high spirits and the drive was fun.

But just outside of Hibbing, we rounded a curve in the highway and approached a huge banner strung across the road. The sign didn't say, "Welcome to Hibbing – Bob Dylan's Hometown" like it should. Instead it said, "Welcome to Hibbing – World's Largest Open Pit Iron Mine."

I knew right then that I had been wrong. The sign was a sign. Well, obviously the sign was a sign. *Anybody* could see that the sign was a *sign*, but *I* could see that the sign was an *omen*. The silver strings would not bring us fame. They would hold no magic. I stared at the vast obscene open pit iron mine and realized that my piercing Joan-Of-Arc-sy vision had been nothing more than a post-Klik hallucination.

Chastened and humiliated, we returned to The Winnie-The-Pooh Capital Of The World.

The End

*   *   *

I played in bands from when I was thirteen until I was forty-two, departing the music scene at various intervals to answer the call of the Ne'er-Do-Well. I played in community clubs, school gyms, church basements, dance halls, concert halls, hotel bars and nightclubs, and

I enjoyed playing in most of those places. But every musician aspires to cutting a record – the permanent archive of a transitory craft. I cut two records. I don't know which caused me the most pain.

I cut my first disc in London, England.

It so happened that one day I was in a crowded London train station, carrying my backpack and sleeping bag. In my pack was my trusty concertina – the squeeze-box made famous by drunken sailors in movies and cartoons. I wasn't what you'd call an accomplished concert concertina-ist, but I could wheeze out a few old standards, and I found it often broke the ice with people.

While bumbling through the crowd in the huge cavernous high-ceilinged echoey train station, I came across an interesting-looking booth. It looked similar to the "four-photos-for-a-quarter" booths that I'd seen in Canada, but this booth had a closeable door on it instead of a curtain, and it was painted all over with musical notes. Intrigued, I moved in to study it more closely. I soon discovered why I'd never seen such a machine before: it was bizarrely British.

The idea was that you go inside, close the door, put in money, wait till the green light goes on, and "sing your greetings" to somebody till the green light goes off. Within a few minutes a 45 RPM record slides out of a slot, packed in a cardboard sleeve, ready for mailing.

So who could resist? I considered my somewhat

limited repertoire and decided on "Camp Town Races," my most polished and accomplished piece.

I followed the instructions and began. The booth was very soundproofed. I couldn't hear the big hum of the crowd outside or the garbled P.A. announcements about trains.

A Sing Your Greetings record is three minutes long. I didn't realize it when I started, but that is a very, very long time. The verse and chorus of "Camp Town Races" are quite short. So when I reached the end, I'd start over again, to get my full money's worth. But to prevent my greetings from getting boring I started singing along with the doo-dah, doo-dah sections, in an always louder and more insane voice, ranging from opera-diva falsetto to Porky Pig (eh-beh-dee, eh-beh-dee DOO-DAH). Finally the green light went off and I desisted.

While I waited for my record to be "released," I opened the door, just in case someone else was out there waiting to sing *their* greetings. But no one was waiting to use the booth, so I sat with my squeeze-box on my lap, lulled by the babbling murmur of the milling crowd.

Suddenly a weird squawking pierced the air. At first neither I nor anyone could tell what it was. The crowd noise dropped as people tried to make sense of the intruding screeching. In horrified shock I suddenly grasped what was going on: *the booth was playing back my "greetings" through speakers on the outside of the booth at a suicidally-embarrassing volume.*

There was absolutely no mention of this phase of the process anywhere in the instructions.

Within a few minutes the whole place had stopped to tune in the wailing audio dementia. People near the booth were pointing at me. Some were laughing. Some looked very scared.

I now know how difficult it is to hold a single thought for three entire minutes.

"I will never see any of these people again."

"I will never see any of these people again."

"I will never see any of these people again...."

My second effort at cutting a record was more carefully planned, but by that time the music scene had degenerated into the music biz – a bizniz in which records make it or break it depending on the size of their promotional budget.

I *had* no promotional budget. Cynthia and I mailed the album out to a few reviewers across the country. The response was good:

"Bartlett's wry humour pokes through his cleverly-worded lyrics. 'Hotel Hell' is a bang-on snapshot of a musician's life on the road, while 'Wall of Noise' includes a defiant band's claim that 'Yeah, we're Top 40 – on a richter scale.'"

Stephen Ostick
The Winnipeg Free Press

"Majors should give a listen to yet another Manitoba-based artist with a lot of talent and ready to break."

> *W.G., The Record Reviewer,*
> *RPM Magazine*
> *Toronto*

"Was I ever blown away from reality with *My Own Bad Self* – excellent tunes! My absolute fave is 'Hotel Hell.'"

> *Lyn Hague, Program Director*
> *CHRW, 94.7 FM London, Ontario*

"I especially enjoyed 'Highway 61 Revisited' and Rex's own 'Hotel Hell.'"

> *Pablo Fairhall, A&R, A&M Records*
> *Toronto*

"By mixing his own tunes in with covers like Dylan's 'Brand New Leopardskin Pillbox Hat' and Leiber and Stoller's 'Saved', Rex shows the strength of his songwriting skills. His lyrical wit and satire in songs like the great 'Hotel Hell' stand well against Dylan in this context. Great fun – and one I'll keep in my collection."

> *Penny Campbell,*
> *Canadian Musician Magazine*
> *Toronto*

"I think 'Hotel Hell' is a great, classic song."

> *Max Hutchinson, A&R, A&M Records*
> *Toronto*

"Bartlett's own pennings display a wry lyrical wit which should be encouraged."

John Kendal
The Winnipeg Sun

"Headingley's Bartlett uses his rough, whiskey soaked voice to great effect on the three original songs and seven covers. The great thing is that all three originals are terrific songs. Bartlett moves from blues to rock to gospel with an infectiously upbeat feel."

Perry Bergson
The Brandon Sun

"Fans of rollicking R & B and grimy well-greased vocals will make the young Manitoban welcome in nightclubs across the country. Bartlett shows enormous promise. For a good time with a new Canadian Bluesman, you can't go wrong with this boisterous introduction."

Helen Metella
The Edmonton Journal

"People do not find their approach boring. Last week, I saw a crowd standing on chairs, screaming for encores, and breaking glasses."

S. Matheson
The Manitoban

"Got lots of requests for Rex's release on the show. Sounds great!"

Holger Petersen, Host,
Saturday Night Blues, CBC

But having good reviews is not the same as having a competitive promotional budget and I looked on as a lot of highly-hyped schlock went gold... then platinum ...then double-platinum.

My album went plywood.

It flopped like a... well, like a disco-dancin' flabby hairless chest.

Do I still sound bitter?

I considered going back to my roots: The Sing Your Greetings label. After all, I reasoned, they offer recording studio, record production and airplay/promotion to a mass audience, all at an affordable price, and at an "instant service" pace. In an eight-hour day at "the station" I figured I could cut a hundred and sixty records. Cynthia could stand outside the booth and flog them. It was an attractive idea. But I lost interest, for once again I could hear the call of the Ne'er-Do-Well. This time it was coming from the South Atlantic Ocean.

Chapter Twenty-Four

Now *That's* Losin' the Ol' Bean

"Tell about the coffee," says Cynthia.

"I don't wanna," says I.

You gotta. I don't gotta. You oughta. Don't hafta. Back and forth until she finally uses it on me: "Aw come *on.*"

You can't argue with logic like that, so, okay, I'll tell about the coffee. After all, I suppose, it *is* a rich source of horror…

Barefoot Cottage came with almost two acres of once-productive land, which became wildly overgrown when the place was abandoned. Now, by Canadian standards, two acres isn't that much land, but on tiny St. Helena (47 square miles) it's like owning Saskatchewan.

And the same gene that compelled us to rescue a crumbling house drove us to try to make the land productive again. So we decided to try growing coffee. We thought it might be a source of some income – just in case the author/poet/artist thing flopped like a disco-dancin' bald pectoral paunch.

A two acre coffee plantation isn't as financially laughable as it sounds, when you consider that St. Helena coffee is the most expensive coffee in the world, selling at ten times the price of ordinary coffee. It is, in fact, *the* most expensive coffee for sale at ultra-snooty *Harrod's*, dahling.

The excellence of St. Helena coffee is long-established. It was awarded First Prize at The London Exhibition in 1851. Today it's a much-sought-after gourmet treat, partly because it's delicious, partly because it's very rare, and partly because the ancient strain of *Coffee Arabica* has remained *pure*, owing to the amazing isolation of St. Helena. In 1733, Green Tipped Bourbon Coffee beans from the coffee port of Mocha, in Yemen, were planted on St. Helena. All the coffee grown on the island today is descended from the 1733 bean.

As a starting point for our coffee growing scheme, Cynthia and I visited a coffee plantation on the other side of the island. The owner was in need of coffee pickers, so we agreed to pick beans in exchange for young trees. What this involved was rising at 2:30 a.m. (can this be why I don't want to remember all this?) and triking at dawn the steep miles to Sandy Bay. Actually, once up and out of my coma, I enjoyed triking on the empty winding road beside the blue, blue ocean, up high mountains, and down through deep valleys filled with lush vegetation, in a beautiful silence broken only by the hum of the trike's tires and birdsong.

At the Sandy Bay plantation, the coffee trees were growing on a steep slope, so even standing required some effort. The method for picking coffee is this: attach a bucket to your chest via a rope around your neck, and pick red beans with both hands at high speed. When the bucket is full, empty it into a gunnysack and repeat and repeat and repeat...

We both found coffee picking addictive and enjoyable. It seems to satisfy some long lost, stifled-by-city-dwelling hunter-gatherer urge. You start picking and soon you've forgotten what your name is. You would answer absently with a grunt if someone called you "Og," and unless you think about it you just *assume* that you live in a nearby cave. The whole hypnotic experience has a way of mentally transporting you way back to a much simpler time.

At the end of the picking day Cynthia and I would load four young coffee trees onto each trike and head home. The weight of four trees, complete with root-ball in wet soil made it feel like large, heartless, flabby disco dancers were sitting behind us on the trikes, dragging their feet on the uphill. We'd crawl into Barefoot Cottage at about 6 p.m, eat fast and then collapse into an instant coma. It always seemed like five minutes later that the alarm clock would attack.

But we amassed one hundred trees through "perseverance" (damage-control-speak for "unrelenting insanity").

This created the opportunity for us to dig one hundred holes – *after* we'd cleared the land. (Can this be why I don't want to remember all this?) We mixed the soil from the holes with compost, refilled the holes, and planted the trees.

At present, there are 850,000 varieties of insect that collectively strip humanity of half its food supply. I mention this only because our coffee trees were instantly attacked by the small, humble, boring-looking hard-backed weevil. Our intention was to grow organic coffee, so, rather than using a pesticide, *we crouched every day, hand picking weevils off each tree.* (Can this be why I don't want to remember all this?) We fought hard but it was a David-and-Goliath thing: two agonized-from-crouching middle-aged humans versus hordes of horny humpin' hungry insects.

Tiny St. Helena is actually a collection of many micro-climates, and we had been warned that coffee won't grow just anywhere on the island. One of the things young coffee trees don't like is wind. Our location wasn't usually windy, *but for some mysterious reason*, giant winds blew in for three days, blackening many leaves. (*By strange coincidence*, at that time, I hadn't yet whupped a certain deceased curse-wielding flab-fondler.)

Our plantation was looking a little worse for wear-and-tear. We, on the other hand, looked like hell for wear-and-tear. The Gods, of course, could see this, and in their mercy, they sent us a way to finish off the trees and put a stop to all this madness. They got someone to advise us that we needed sheep to mow the grass between the trees.

Neither Cynthia nor I knew anything at all about sheep. You may not either. I will share what we learned.

Sheep are what's known as "livestock." They are not what's known as "pets." Livestock differ from pets thusly: If you build a nice house for livestock, and put lots of clean hay on the floor to make a nice soft bed for them, unlike pets, livestock will come in and just poo all over it. "Oh lovely," you say. "Charming," you say. "Where ya gonna sleep now?" you ask your livestock. They lie down right there in the filth. "Right here," they say. "*What?*" they say.

Sheep come in two forms: "rams" and "ewes" ("boy" and "girl" would be much too simple; everybody loves techno-jargon these days). We bought two rams. Although ewes do not ewe each other, by curious coincidence, rams actually do ram each other. Hard. Which makes a sickening, coconut-cracking sound. It's awful to watch. They are powerful animals, and they stand staring at each other like steroid-crazed wrestlers waiting for the commercial break to end. Then they leap forward, violently smashing their heads together. On impact, their brains slap around inside their skulls, leaving them momentarily mentally blank. Science is still trying to determine whether or not a "tilt" sign appears inside their heads, and, if it does, whether or not rams can read it. Finally the little blob of grey matter settles, permitting rams to think "duh." And then, "Hey, let's do that again!"

Our rams enjoyed this until they'd busted off each other's horns and their heads were bleeding. We saw this as a problem and solved it by giving one ram away to a neighbour. But all we'd really done was create a different problem. Deprived of a proper ramming partner, our remaining ram was forced to find a substitute – us. (Can this be why I don't want to remember all this?)

After Cynthia had been pin-wheeled down the hill we traded our ram for a ewe. She was gentle and tame, and had a beautiful long-nosed face and a lovely singing voice. We named her "Baa-aa-aabs." She stood on her hind legs as a greeting and good-naturedly accepted the two mynah birds that rode on her back all day pretending to be circus performers.

But Baa-aa-aabs liked coffee. And she managed, by various devious and clever means, to finish off our coffee plantation, one tree at a time. There. That's the whole sad, sordid story. I hope you're happy now, Cynthia.

I'm off to make myself a cup of coffee.

Instant.

Can this be why I don't want to remember all this?

Epilogue

My pen is weary. My arm is weary. My bum is weary. I can tell that I've neared the end of my humble narrative. And soon it will be time to bundle these pages into an envelope and put them on the ship in the hope that somewhere out in The Big World there are readers eagerly awaiting a book that has survived being cursed.

Darkness falls quickly in the tropics. Right now I'm sitting quietly in the brief evening twilight, listening to the bawling hee-haw of a neighbour's donkey and the crowing of roosters and the frogs and crickets as they tune up for the evening wail-a-thon.

Sometimes I sit here in our cement shack and think about where in the world I am and where in the world I've come from. I contemplate the fact that for five years now I have not shovelled snow. For me, this is an undeniable victory. And yet some perverse and stubborn lobe of my brain often insists on remembering snow with *nostalgia*. Why? Why must I, at odd moments, achingly recall my aluminum toboggan with the yellow rope? *Rosebud! ROSEBUD!*

Sorry about that. I'm back. I'm perfectly all right. I'm fine. Apart from the occasional, unavoidable, homesick-for-Canada freak-outs I'm completely okay.

Usually I have no problem accepting our low-budget one-way-ticket anti-winterist exile, because I think Cynthia and I have pretty much found what we set out looking for – a spectacularly beautiful warm place where a walk is an unforgettable scenic delight. And also a pleasure, as there are no mosquitos or biting insects to speak of, and no snakes or dangerous beasties. This island is a walker's paradise.

And swimming here in the warm, clear, blue-green ocean is a joy. Cynthia and I dive in from the steps of the wharf in Jamestown and swim among schools of brilliantly-coloured tropical fish – no sharks. St. Helena's marine environment offers so much – from sport fishing and dolphin watching, to snorkeling and scuba diving in James Bay along "underwater trails" to visit shipwrecks from three different centuries.

The weather here is good. Unlike many places with a temperate climate, St. Helena experiences no hurricanes or tornados. Although it rains sometimes, there's no lightning or thunder. A middle-aged Saint told me she remembers that when she was a kid, school was cancelled one day because thunder was heard out at sea.

The Saints are generally a down-home friendly bunch. Most people wave an amiable greeting whether they know you or not. They project a pleasant old-fashioned civility and politeness, often calling people "Sir" or "Ma'am".

The island still has a simple, old-time charm.

Telephone numbers are only four digits long. There is no building over three stories high. Many people here, us included, cook on a cast-iron woodstove, and you can still see people bringing home firewood by donkey.

There are interesting antique words and phrases still in daily use on St. Helena. People say stuff like, "Us can see way over yonder with these new spectacles." And one day, I saw something here that I never thought I'd see anywhere. I watched a white-haired Saint perform a time-worn ritual: he lit his hand-rolled cigarette with a *tinderbox*.

I like how St. Helena still *feels* so connected to its fascinating past. So much of the island remains unchanged from the days of sailing ships. There are areas here where you can turn a full circle and not see any man-made structure. Perched high on cliffs around the island are old stone forts and gun batteries, complete with cast-iron cannons. Hiking to a remote coastal gun battery is an excellent day's outing, and as you sit there looking out at the same giant empty sea that a British soldier guarding Napoleon would have seen, listening to the same sea-bird calls, and viewing the same un-developed rugged coastline, you just can't help but *feel* the history.

On rare occasions here, an odd muffled whuffling sound can be heard. People run from their houses and look up. And if we're lucky, those of us with good eyesight can sometimes see a speck moving between distant cloud banks high above us. A noteworthy event. We have seen a *plane* on its way to South America from Africa. As the sound fades out and the excitement recedes, the neighbours go back to what they were doing... while I fall to my knees sobbing and shrieking at the empty sky, "Come back! I'm down *here!* Pleeeeze come back! *I WANNA GO TOBOGGANIIIIIIIIING!*"

But not to worry. These little aching-for-Canada "outages" (as I call them) are brief – often lasting only a day or two – and I usually have no more than one or two a week. So I'm fine. Really. Just fine.

It's getting quite dark now, here at the kitchen table.

I'm going to sign off before I have to light the paraffin lamp. But before I go I want to say that I hope you've enjoyed your armchair tour through this curious little world. And I hope you'll come see St. Helena for yourself. It's the perfect place – especially now that the curse has been lifted.

Did I mention that The British Government is going to build an international airport here, operational by 2010?

There you are, you see. *Proof* that the curse has been lifted, isn't it.

...Isn't it?

Bibliography

Ashmole, Philip and Myrtle. *St. Helena and Ascension Island: A Natural History*. Oswestry, England: Anthony Nelson, 2000.

Aubry, Octave. *St. Helena*. London: Victor Gollancz Ltd., 1937.

Baker, Ian. *St. Helena: One Man's Island*. Berkshire, England: Wilton 65, 2004.

Barnett, Corralli. *Bonaparte*. London: George Allen and Unwin Ltd., 1978.

Bennett, George Brooks. *Reminiscences of George Brooks Bennett 1816 – 1886*. (unpublished) courtesy of Basil and Barbara George, St. Helena Island.

Bertrand, H.G. *Napoleon at St. Helena: Memoirs of General Bertrand, January to May 1821*. London: Cassell and Company Ltd., 1953.

Blackburn, Julia. *The Emperor's Last Island*. London: Secker and Warburg, 1991.

George, Barbara B. *Jacob's Ladder*. Bristol, England: Printsetters, 1995.

Gosse, Philip. *St. Helena 1502 – 1938*. Shropshire, England: Anthony Nelson Ltd., 1990.

Hibbert, Christopher. *Napoleon: His Wives and Women*. London: Harper Collins, 2002.

Kauffmann, Jean-Paul. *The Dark Room At Longwood*. London: Harvill Press, 1997.

Kemble, James. *Gorrequer's Diary, St. Helena During Napoleon's Exile*. London: Heinemann, 1969.

Marryat, Frederick. *The Little Savage*. #137 Classics Illustrated Comics. New York: Gilberton Company Inc., 1957.

Mathieson, Ian and Carter, Lawrence. *Exploring St. Helena: A Walker's Guide*. Shropshire, England: Anthony Nelson Ltd., 1992.

McCulloch, Neil. *A guide to the birds of St. Helena and Ascension Island*. Bedfordshire, England: The Royal Society for the Protection of Birds, 2004.

Moorehead, Alan. *Darwin and the Beagle*. New York: Harper and Row, 1969.

O'Meara, Barry. *Napoleon In Exile or a Voice from St. Helena*. Two Volumes. London, 1822.

Weaver, Barry. *A Guide To The Geology Of Saint Helena*. Norman, Oklahoma: University of Oklahoma, 1991.

Some fishing information and some historical dates courtesy of The Jamestown Tourist Office

Some information about endemics on St. Helena from the World Wildlife website: www.worldwildlife.org

*   *   *

The following websites offer more information about St. Helena and some nice photos of the island :
www.sthelenatourism.com
www.sthelena.se/tour/index.htm

For information about travelling to St. Helena on the RMS *St. Helena* see: www.rms-st-helena.com
or contact Andrew Weir Shipping by email at:
reservations@aws.co.uk
or contact the St. Helena Line in Cape Town at:
sthelenaline@mweb.co.za

For information about ICE trikes: www.ice.hpv.co.uk

Did you borrow this book?

If you want to order a copy for yourself,
go to:

www.toppermostbooks.ca